A MATCH MADE IN HEAVEN

ALSO BY ZEV CHAFETS

Members of the Tribe
The Project
Hang Time
The Bookmakers
Inherit the Mob
Devil's Night: And Other True Tales of Detroit
Heroes and Hustlers, Hard Hats and Holy Men
Double Vision

A MATCH MADE IN HEAVEN

American Jews, Christian Zionists,

and One Man's Exploration of

the Weird and Wonderful

Judeo-Evangelical Alliance

ZEV CHAFETS

HarperCollins*Publishers*

HarperCollins books may be purchased for educational, business, or sales promotional use. For information, please write: Special Markets Department, Harper-Collins Publishers, 10 East 53rd Street, New York, NY 10022.

FIRST EDITION

Designed by Joseph Rutt

Library of Congress Cataloging-in-Publication Data is available.

ISBN: 978-0-06-089058-2
ISBN-10: 0-06-089058-4

07 08 09 10 11 ID/RRD 10 9 8 7 6 5 4 3 2 1

For June McGinn, my hero's hero.
And for Ella, my baby's baby.

CONTENTS

PART THREE

AFTERWORD: WARTIME

PART ONE

AMONG THE CHRISTIANS

ONE

JEWS FOR JESUS

I've been keeping a sharp eye on Christians ever since an eleven-year-old first baseman named Monroe informed me that I, one of the Chosen People, would be going to hell when I died. It wasn't a threat, or a recruiting pitch. He didn't care. It was just a piece of information he had picked up at the Emmanuel Baptist Church Sunday school, in Pontiac, Michigan. We were Little League teammates, and he figured I should know.

The warning seemed absurd to me. I went to school with Christians. They were my neighbors. I learned to ride my bike in the parking lot of the Grace Lutheran Church, across the street from my house. The house was built by my grandfather in the 1930s, a place where my mother grew up before me. There were very few Jews around during my childhood. Mostly I knew Christians, and it had never occurred to me that, dead or alive, they were going someplace I wasn't.

Naturally I knew that Christians came in different varieties. The Sicilian kids went to Catholic school and put ashes on their heads every year around Easter. I saw different preachers on television on Sunday mornings, too. Oral Roberts was my favorite; I loved the way he pounded people on the skull, healing them in the name of Jesus and issuing dire threats to the unsaved. I regarded this as entertainment, plain and simple, something along the lines of pro wrestling.

But after Monroe's warning, I became interested in Emmanuel Baptist Church, and the more I leaned, the more interested I got. I found out it had its own football team, the Crusaders. The pastor, Reverend Tom Malone, owned a personal airplane—more than enough to qualify him as a celebrity in the Pontiac of the 1950s. In the summer, Malone held tent revivals in the empty lot next to his church. Sometimes I'd cruise by on my bike, just to hear the muffled shouting and singing going on inside. I didn't venture in myself, but I put it on my list of future adventures.

I was in high school when a traveling evangelist named Hyman Appleman came to town. He was a Russian-born Jew who found Jesus in Denver in 1925. I heard him tell his story on the local radio station in a Yiddish accent and I was determined to enter the big top and see him for myself.

I enlisted a friend, Jim Embree, as a guide. He was an Episcopalian who had never been to a Baptist revival in his life, but I figured he'd have some idea what to do. I figured he would give me a little cover, and possibly even some tent cred.

Appleman preached that night in his comical brogue, telling mildly sarcastic anecdotes at the expense of the Chosen People. My fellow worshippers guffawed, and I laughed right along with them. He struck me as a buffoon. Only later did I learn he was a world-famous evangelist and an early influence on Billy Graham. "Thousands of names are written in the Lamb's Book of Life because Dr. Appleman passed their way," Graham has remarked.

Appleman finished his stem-winder and instructed the congregation to close their eyes. "If there is anyone here who hasn't been saved by the Lord Jesus, I want him to raise his hand," he said. My friend showed his Protestant smarts by keeping his hands in his lap. I raised mine. I didn't know that spotters were deployed throughout the crowd. By the time I opened my eyes they were on me, half a dozen hyperexcited Baptists imploring me to come forward and accept Jesus. I tried to politely refuse but they didn't want to hear it. Someone handed me a little information card and a ballpoint. I could picture an evangelical posse turning up at my house the next day if I filled it out. So I did what any young. self-respecting Jew would have done—I wrote down the name and address of the local rabbi and hotfooted it out of the tent. I wasn't saved that night, but I came closer than any Chafets ever had, and I found the foray into foreign territory exhilarating.

MICHIGAN IN THOSE days was a great place for a kid with an eye for exotic religious practitioners. I became a devotee of Prophet Jones, the ecstatic black spiritualist preacher who wore a crown and an ermine robe, spoke directly to Jesus on a disconnected telephone during Sunday night services, sometimes threatened to strike inattentive members of his congregation dead, and gave sermons with titles such as "God Don't Like Women." Eventually the Prophet was run out of Detroit by the vice squad for what was then regarded as illicit sexual activity, leaving behind a fifty-four-room mansion painted blue, a closet of expensive outfits, and a coterie of passionate admirers.

Father Charles Coughlin was another favorite of mine. During the Depression he had been a nationally famous radio preacher who specialized in railing against Jewish communists, bankers, and warmongers (1930s versions of the euphemism "neocon"). Coughlin's followers marched in the streets of Detroit chanting, "Send the Jews back where they came from in leaky boats."

World War II was hard on Father Coughlin. He bet on fascism and lost. By the time I caught up with him, in the 1960s, he was a spent force, a red-faced old priest who looked like he would be willing to drink hair tonic. I made it a point of attending Christmas mass at his Shrine of the Little Flower in Royal Oak in suburban Detroit. I'd sit in the rear of the huge church and think, 'This guy would drop dead if he knew I was in the audience."

Around this time a local Reform rabbi named Sherwin Wine announced that he didn't believe in God and that he was starting a congregation for Jewish atheists. This seemed perfectly natural to me. Most of the Jews I knew in Pontiac were Reform Jews. Their denomination (and mine) in those days was almost entirely about civil rights. We didn't speak to one another about God. Our prayers, such as they were, consisted primarily of reflections on an abstract being who resembled Franklin D. Roosevelt. The Bible was second-rate Shakespeare. To the extent we read it at all, we concentrated on those prophets whose teachings were in line with Pete Seeger. The Holocaust was never discussed. Israel was a foreign country.

I was a sophomore at the University of Michigan in May 1967, when Egypt closed the Straits of Tiran and mobilized troops in the Sinai. This was an obvious act of war intended to choke Israel's most vulnerable shipping lane. Even from my distant perch, it was pretty clear there would have to be a response. I heard military analysts on television predicting that Israel would lose an all-out fight with the Egyptians and their Arab allies. I read in the papers that Israeli citizens were being called into the military reserves and teenagers were digging mass graves in Tel Aviv.

One day I got a call from a friend in Massachusetts, Eric Yoffie. We had known each other from camp, and we were both active in the National Federation of Temple Youth. Eric said that the Jewish Agency, a group I had never heard of, was signing up volunteers to take the place of Israelis called up to fight.

Eric was going. Did I want to come too? To my surprise, I did.

I passed a mandatory physical and bought a trunkload of surplus gear suitable for a safari from Joe's Army and Navy. We were scheduled to take off on June 5. That morning the war broke out and we were bumped off our flight by returning Israeli reservists. By the time we were rescheduled, the fighting was all over. They don't call it the Six-Day War for nothing.

I got to Israel anyway, two months later, as a junior year abroad student at the Hebrew University in Jerusalem. My goal was to learn a little Hebrew and maybe pick up a few Jewish customs. I expected to be in Israel for an academic year, but within a month I knew I was staying permanently.

I had my reasons. Some were pretty trivial: I loved Jerusalem's mild weather and the girls were sexy. Others were more grandiose: I was thrilled and honored, in the self-centered way only an American baby boomer could be, to find myself a member of the first generation in two thousand years to live in a Jewish country. All this for me! I was also delighted to learn that you didn't have to be a nice Jewish boy to be a Jew in good standing. Some Americans were put off by the rough manners and macho posturing of Israelis, but I loved being in a place where the Jews got to be the gentiles.

It was in Jerusalem that year that I saw, for the first time in my life, men and women with concentration camp numbers on their arms. I had been raised to consider Hitler from an American perspective—a wartime enemy. Suddenly I took the Nazis personally. It seemed wrong that people who had gone through the camps could again be in mortal danger, twenty years later. I began to feel that the fight for Israel, like the fight for racial integration in the United States, was an obviously moral cause. I was embarrassed to leave it to the children of the people with the numbers on their arms.

•   •   •

I WAS IN Israel in 1969, when I got drafted by the American army. I had two choices: go back and serve or stay in Israel. Draft evasion was a federal crime punishable by $10,000 and five years in prison. Since there had never been any amnesties for draft dodgers, I figured that whatever I decided would be a lifelong choice.

I loved America. My family was there, and in the days before direct-dial telephone and the Internet, Israel was, in my mother's mordant phrase, "in Asia." Israel had the economy of a Warsaw Pact nation and a standard of living to match. Musically, it was still behind the Irving Berlin Wall. The only sport was kickball (known to the rest of the world as soccer). I had no job, no close relatives, no profession, and no prospects. I barely spoke the language. Who could resist?

I wrote to my draft board in Pontiac and said, "Sorry." Instead, I served in the Israeli army. I didn't exactly tip the balance of power in the Middle East, but I felt I was doing something important in a place where I was needed.

The Palestinian issue was just becoming trendy, and some of my Jewish friends at the University of Michigan had a hard time understanding my decision. Why would I want to live in a country the Black Panthers didn't approve of? How could I fight Arabs? Weren't they on the same revolutionary side as the Vietcong?

I was never bothered by this particular scruple. The way I saw it (and still do), the Arabs had a lot of legitimate grievances, and if I were an Arab myself I'd probably be on the Arab side. But I was a Jew. Besides, I didn't think the Arabs had behaved very well, starting with their invasion of Israel at its inception in 1948. You have to be a special kind of jerk to attack people fresh out of the concentration camps, no matter how upset you are with the idea of living next to them.

The big issue when I first came to Israel was the future of the territories Israel conquered in the Six-Day War, but the biblical lands of Judea and Samaria had no special religious or emotional meaning to me. If the Arabs wanted them back in return for peace, fine. If they didn't—and they made that clear at an Arab League summit in the fall of 1967 by declaring a policy of "no negotiation, no recognition and no peace" that they didn't—that was fine, too. I was raised during the cold war and I took protracted conflicts more or less in stride.

Besides, I couldn't really buy into the Israeli left's notion that giving back the territories to the Arabs was a moral imperative. I noticed that a lot of the Israelis making this argument lived in houses or on kibbutzim that had belonged to Arabs before 1948. Many had businesses that relied on cheap Arab labor. Still, hypocrisy isn't a capital crime, and I was too busy getting acclimated in my new country to worry about mere ideology.

Meanwhile, back in the States, the FBI was now officially on my case. When agents staged a surprise inspection on Christmas Eve, my mother helpfully informed them that we were Jews and that it would be much more sensible to search for me on Passover. That way the agents could spend next Christmas with their families. When I heard this I had to laugh. My mother was too American to be mean to the FBI. On the other hand, she knew damn well that I wasn't going to try to sneak into Michigan to attend a family seder.

AFTER FINISHING THE army, I answered an ad in the newspaper and landed a job with the Liberal Party, the junior partner in what was to become the Likud. The Liberals were a secular petit bourgeois faction with no ideology greater than tax avoidance. Issues of war and peace were left to the senior partner, Herut, and its leader, Menachem Begin. Begin had run for prime minister in every election since 1949, and lost every time. No one expected a different outcome in the future.

When Begin won the 1977 election, there were more senior government positions than Likudniks to fill them. I was appointed director of the Government Press Office, a position that was something like the White House director of communications. I was twenty-nine years old.

As the only American on Begin's staff, I was occasionally consulted on issues relating to my native country—especially after it became clear that the Israeli embassy in Washington, staffed by holdovers from the Labor years, wasn't being very helpful. One of the things I was asked about was Christian Zionists—evangelicals like Jerry Falwell and Pat Robertson, who wanted to establish relations with the government of Israel.

I wasn't particularly enthusiastic. To me, these Christian Zionists were evangelists like Pontiac's Reverend Tom Malone. But Israel didn't suffer from an overabundance of friends, and gradually I began to see that Christian Zionists were politically useful, even if their hypersincerity was a bit off-putting.

I don't mean to suggest that my opinion was in any way crucial. Menachem Begin liked evangelicals from the start. They believed, as he did, that the Bible gave Israel a deed to the Holy Land. They supported his policies. And they were willing to go to the mat for him against Jimmy Carter over the issue of Jewish settlements in the West Bank and Gaza.

Begin's office became a destination for visiting Christian Zionist celebrities. One day Johnny Cash and June Carter came by for a photo op. Cash was a lover of biblical history and came to see Begin directly from a visit to Masada, the mountain fortress where Jewish zealots had, two thousand years earlier, staged a sort of

kosher Alamo in their futile rebellion against the Roman con-
querors of Palestine. The early Zionists adopted Masada as a
symbol of steadfastness and courage. When Cash told Begin he
had been there, the prime minister slammed his hand down on
his desk and proclaimed, "Masada will never fall again!" The Man
in Black was so startled he nearly jumped out of his cowboy
boots.

The American Jewish leadership was scandalized and outraged
by the company Begin was keeping. Most of the Jewish grandees
were liberals who had never met an evangelical Christian and
didn't want to. They disagreed with Begin's settlement policy and
saw (correctly) that it would lead to a clash with the Carter administration. They were also put off by Begin's European looks
and Jewish mannerisms. The Jews of New York and Los Angeles
wanted Sabra heroes like the dashing, one-eyed warrior Moshe
Dayan. Begin reminded them of their uncle Louie in dry goods.

This didn't bother the evangelicals a bit. Begin suited their
notion of what a Jewish prime minister ought to be. He called
them "Reverend" and swapped Old Testament quotes with them.
The prime minister was a man who divided the world into three
parts: Us (the Jews), Them (the gentiles), and Me. He didn't
judge Christians by where they went to college, their rural ac-
cents, or, for that matter, what political party they belonged to (at
this stage, the late 1970s, many, including Pat Robertson, were
still Democrats, although they were quickly trending Republican).
The Christian Zionists supported Begin's policies, and that was
enough.

IN THE SUMMER of 1982, Israel invaded Lebanon. I supported
the war and defended it to the international press. The PLO had

created an armed, hostile ministate on Israel's northern border (just as Hezbollah did a generation later), and having grown up a bridge away from Canada, I believed that sovereign states had a right to expect peace and quiet from their neighbors.

The Christians of Lebanon were allies of Israel in the war, and Begin was happy to have them. They were impressive fellows, but unfortunately, Begin overestimated their fighting spirit and underestimated their hatred of the Palestinians. After Israel conquered Beirut in the late summer of 1982, Christian militiamen massacred Palestinian Muslims in the Sabra and Shatila refugee camps.

Israel was blamed for this, and rightly so: occupying powers have the obligation to protect civilians. But Begin bitterly resented the charge that he was responsible. "Christians murder Muslims and they blame the Jews," he said. "This is a blood libel."

This sounded self-pitying and false to me. It certainly wasn't a position I wanted to defend to journalists. And so I quit.

For the next decade I wrote books and helped found the *Jerusalem Report*. It was at the magazine's first anniversary party that I met Lisa Beyer. She was the new *Time* bureau chief in Jerusalem. One thing led to another. We fell in love and decided to get married.

Lisa isn't Jewish. Her mother is a very lapsed Cajun Catholic, her father a born-again Pentecostal who once spoke in tongues on Jim Bakker's *Praise the Lord* television show. When the time came to fly down to her hometown, Lafayette, Louisiana, to meet the family, I felt like Woody Allen on the way to visit Annie Hall's grandmother.

That weekend, two of Lisa's elderly Cajun aunts happened to be visiting. Although it is not the custom in Lafayette to discuss politics at the dinner table, the aunts talked about the upcoming gubernatorial race. Both, it turned out, were planning to vote for David Duke, the former head of the Louisiana Ku Klux Klan. They were mad at Duke's opponent, Edwin Edwards, over some arcane local issue, but still, rooting for Duke struck me as rather extreme. Lisa was amused by my attempt to nod my way through the conversation, but I thought I covered up pretty well.

After dinner the aunts announced that they would teach me *bourré,* a Cajun card game. As we sat down at the kitchen table, one suddenly called to Lisa's mom, "June, bring in the sheet."

The sheet? What was this, some sort of Klan game? "What do you need a sheet for?" I asked.

"You put it down when the table's sticky," said one. I saw they were grinning. They had seen *Annie Hall,* too.

The next day we went to meet Lisa's father. As we settled down in his living room I pointed to a picture of the Western Wall in Jerusalem that hung over the mantel. "Reminds me of home," I said.

Lisa's dad didn't know we were planning to get married but he had his suspicions. "Since you live in Israel, am I right in assuming that you're a Jewish fella?" he asked.

"Yes."

There was a pause. A long pause, it seemed to me. Then he said, "It is my belief that the Jews are God's Chosen People."

"Well, sir," I said, "in that case I've got some very good news for you about your future grandchildren."

Lisa and I spent nine years in Israel and then moved to the United States. It was a deal we had made before our wedding— stay until my eldest son, Shmulik, entered the army, then go to New York so Lisa could continue her career. I joked that it was a triumph of feminism over Zionism but I was very unhappy about leaving. A consolation was that, in August 2000, Israel appeared to be in the final stages of making peace with the Palestinians.

We bought a house in Pelham, New York, a Westchester suburb popular with journalists and literary types. We had decided to raise our two children as Jews, which meant joining a synagogue. When I called the Pelham Jewish Center, a Conservative synagogue, the rabbi informed me that we wouldn't be welcome. The Conservative movement, he explained, follows the rule of Talmudic Judaism: only the offspring of a Jewish mother are born kosher. Our kids, with a gentile mother, are ipso facto goyim. He suggested I join a Reform temple, where they aren't so choosy about racial bloodlines. I did.

I SAW THE attack on the World Trade Center and the Pentagon through Israeli eyes, as part of a worldwide jihad. My neighbors and friends didn't see it that way. Some viewed it as a discrete act of terrorism, like Timothy McVeigh's bombing in Oklahoma City. Others felt that the United States had it coming. At a party not long after the attack, a friend took me aside and warned me that people—by which he meant liberal Christians like himself—were starting to grumble about American support for Israel. The Bush administration *was* very committed to Israel, wasn't it? And weren't some of the Bush advisers, well, neocons? You could see how that might upset the Arabs. Maybe a more balanced American policy would help straighten things out.

The main culprit, as far as my friends were concerned, was George W. Bush, followed closely by Republican Christians. Wasn't Osama Bin Laden just a bearded version of Pat Robertson? And did you hear that Jerry Falwell blamed the attack on American promiscuity and immorality? The fact that Falwell and Robertson and the other Christian fundamentalists were on *their* side of what Bin Laden called "the jihad against Jews and crusaders" didn't seem to register with many liberal Jews. As far as they were

concerned, the real enemy was George W. Bush and his fundamentalist supporters.

Lisa and I were invited to the fiftieth birthday party of a close
friend. The party was held in a cozy Riverdale inn. Most of the
guests were journalists, writers, and academics; many were very
successful and quite well known. Almost everyone there was
Jewish, a fact commented upon by each of the few gentiles who
rose to give a toast.

As for the Jews, they mostly mixed their tributes to the birthday
boy with insults directed against the recently reelected George W.
Bush.

We sat next to a married couple, a pair of high-powered academic psychologists affiliated with a prestigious New York university, who loudly applauded every dig at the president. "It's
frightening to realize that this man was elected," the woman said
to me. "What kind of person would vote for him?"

A few weeks earlier I had cast a ballot, for the first time in my
life, in an American presidential election. I voted for Bush and I
told her so.

She and her husband looked at me in amazement. How could
a Bush voter have infiltrated the party? Was this some sort of gro-
tesque joke? Finally the woman said, "I refuse to believe that!"

"A lot of people voted for Bush," I said mildly. "Sixty million
and change."

"Not Jews," she snapped. "A Jew who voted for George Bush is a
Jew for Jesus."

Lisa was smiling. She is often taken to be Jewish and, as a result,
has had quite an education about what liberal Jews say to each
other when they think gentiles aren't listening.

"My parents are Holocaust survivors," added the woman, as if
this clinched the argument.

"Sorry to hear it," I said, which, I immediately realized, might be subject to interpretation. The husband saw the conversation heading off the cliff and intervened.

"It's just that we've never met anyone who voted for Bush," he said in the fake nonjudgmental tone of a man who deals professionally with psychopaths. "We're really interested. It would be fascinating to talk to you more about this, to see how your mind works."

"Yeah, that would really be something," I said. I could just picture these two in laboratory coats, peering deep into my eyes to find the gleam of perversity that would compel me, an Israeli and a Jew, to vote for the most pro-Israeli, pro-Jewish president in American history.

"What could you possibly find to like about Bush? He's a fundamentalist Christian," said the woman. "He wants to start Armageddon!"

I had been hearing variations on this theme from friends and family for the past few years. They, like the shrinks, couldn't fathom how I could tolerate, much less support, a born-again Christian like George W. Bush, or think a positive thought about Jerry Falwell. I understood them well enough. I myself am constantly infuriated by Israeli rabbinical politicians who act morally superior and want to impose their religious views on society at large. But the intifada (and, subsequently, 9/11, the rise of Hamas and Hezbollah, and the threat of Iranian nuclear weapons) shifted my priorities.

Evangelical Christians—led by George W. Bush—were offering an alliance with Israel and its American Jewish supporters based on what they were calling "Judeo-Christian" values. Liberal Jews were disinclined to accept this offer because it would mean tolerating, if not supporting, the evangelical domestic agenda and cultural style. Maybe in peacetime I would have been, too. It is more emotionally satisfying to fight the Falwells than to join them.

But this isn't peacetime. And, no matter how often Jewish liberals declare that the United States isn't a Christian country, that is exactly what it is. Jews make up less than 2 percent of the population—an influential percent, to be sure, but still, a tiny minority. The bargain extended by the evangelicals—to add "Judeo" to the name of the firm—is not easily dismissed.

Like all offers of partnership, this one needs to be weighed in terms of its costs and benefits. For Israel, the gains are obvious, even though some liberal Jews try very hard to make it look like a bad deal. In her 2006 book, *Kingdom Coming: The Rise of Christian Nationalism,* Michelle Goldberg, a young American journalist who describes herself as a Jewish secular humanist, asserted that "the alliance between Christian Zionists and the most fanatical Israeli settlers is well known." But like many things that are well known, it doesn't happen to be true.

The evangelical-Israeli alliance is not a pact between Christian and Israeli religious nuts. It is a well-established relationship between the leaders of evangelical American Christianity and *mainstream* Israel. Every prime minister since Begin has relied on the support of the Christian right. Ehud Barak, the last Labor Party prime minister, is actually listed as a member of the faculty at Pat Robertson's Regent University (the only unsaved member, as far as I could discover).

The dislike and contempt for evangelical Christians that is so integral to American Jewish cultural and political thinking is almost wholly absent in Israel. A few very reactionary Orthodox rabbis object to any connection with goyim. A few Israeli leftists whose views are in constant conformity with Western fashion hate Zionist Christians mostly because the *New York Review of Books* does. But the average Israeli—even the average anticlerical secular Israeli like me—appreciates evangelical support.

For American Jews, who tend to deny that they are in any way personally threatened by the jihad, the issue is obviously more clouded. But it should be said that if Jews feel entirely safe in the United States, it is because they are wrapped in the larger American polity. If the conservative Christians they believe to be anti-Semites actually *were* anti-Semites, life wouldn't seem so secure to them.

It is also worth considering what would happen if the U.S. government were to actually decide—as some on the Pat Buchanan right as well as the Ramsey Clark left argue—that supporting Israel, with its paltry 6 million people, isn't worth alienating the billion plus Muslims. Do American Jews really want to make the case for Israel all by themselves, without support of Christian Zionists? And, do they believe they can continue to count on this support as they position themselves as the chief adversaries of evangelical cultural and political aspirations?

It is clear from every poll and survey that no community in the United States is more *philo*-Semitic than conservative Christians. Most Jews are, by now, aware of this, but find it impossible to believe. They can't get past two thousand years of Christian persecution and two hundred years of secular liberalism. Many believe that evangelicals want to convert them, or to use them as cannon fodder in some great End of Days Armageddon battle. They suspect that behind the warm, toothy smiles of the evangelicals is a coldhearted desire to establish a Christian theocracy in the United States. When they get to thinking about rural folk their minds go—as mine did on my first meeting with Lisa's aunts—to white sheets and burning crosses.

I understand the skepticism. And, during the year I spent among evangelicals, I kept an eye out—the same critical eye I have been casting on Christians since my Little League days in Pontiac.

What I found was that Evangelical Christians, for reasons of their own, are, in an unprecedented way, extending a hand of friendship and wartime alliance to Jews; and the ancient tribal instinct to slap that hand away is a dangerous one. It may be that American Jews will decide they would rather face the jihad alone than rely on conservative Christians. But if they do, it is a decision that will come at great cost to their connection to Israel and their relationship with tens of millions of their fellow Americans. It is not a choice that ought to be made based on stereotypes, knee-jerk partisanship, or simple prejudice. Christian Zionism, in a time of jihad, deserves a closer look.

IN THE BEGINNING

Protestant philo-Semitism got off the *Mayflower.* The Pilgrims saw their voyage to the New World as a reprise of the exodus from Egypt. They adopted Old Testament laws, gave their children and their settlements Hebrew names, and taught the Bible in their schools and universities. For a wild moment they even considered making Hebrew the language of the New World, an initiative that foundered on the first Puritan attempt to pronounce the throat-scraping Hebrew letter *chet.* Writing came easier. The shield of Yale University is inscribed Urim v'Thummim ("light and truth"), a phrase from the book of Exodus.

The first actual Jews in the colonies, a group of twenty-three refugees fleeing the Portuguese Inquisition in Brazil, arrived in New Amsterdam in 1654. The Dutch governor, Peter Stuyvesant, who did not share the English Puritans' taste for Hebrews, wanted to expel the lot, but intervention by the Jewish investors of the Dutch West Indian Company saved them—the first example of Jewish lobbying in the New World.

There were about two thousand Jews in America at the time of the Declaration of Independence. Most were Sephardim, Jews of Portuguese or Spanish origin who came to the colonies by way of Holland or England. Some settled in Savannah, Charleston, and other southern ports, but the majority, even then, lived in the cities of the Northeast.

A number of Jews fought in the Revolutionary War, none more disastrously than Francis Salvador, who, at the head of a frontier force in Georgia on July 1, 1776, had the misfortune of encountering a band of pro-British Creek Indians, who promptly scalped him.

The most famous Jewish patriot was Haym Solomon, a Philadelphia financier who loaned the Continental Congress a fortune, got stiffed, and died broke. But the loyalty of Solomon, Salvador, and other Jewish revolutionaries gave standing in the new republic. In 1790, President George Washington himself dispatched a letter to the Jews of Newport, Rhode Island. "May the children of the stock of Abraham who dwell in the land continue to merit and enjoy the goodwill of the other inhabitants," he wrote.

It doesn't seem like much today but that letter sent a welcoming signal to the Jews of Europe. Immigrants began arriving, most of them from Germany. They didn't necessarily see themselves as the "seed of Abraham" or, in the words of Haym Solomon, members of the "Hebrew nation." They wanted to be regular Americans of the Jewish faith. In 1841, at the dedication of the Reform temple of Charleston, South Carolina, Rabbi Gustav Posnanski put it into words: "This country," he proclaimed, "is our Palestine, this city our Jerusalem, this house of God our Temple."

Forty years later, this attitude was challenged by the emergence of a proto-Zionist movement. Groups of young Eastern European Jews, called Chovevei Zion ("Lovers of Zion") began moving to Palestine and establishing agricultural colonies. This excited the interest and support of several European benefactors, chief among them the Rothschild family, but American Jews didn't like the looks of it. In 1885, the dominant Reform movement published a strong anti-Zionist statement: "We consider ourselves no longer a nation but a religious community; and we therefore expect neither a return to Palestine, nor a sacrificial worship under the sons of Aaron, nor the restoration of any of the laws concerning a Jewish state." Orthodox Jews, a minority within the American Jewish community at the time, *did* expect a restoration, but considered the idea of building a secular Jewish state to be heretical.

Some Christians saw it differently. To them, the return of the Jews to the Holy Land was a sign that biblical prophecy was being fulfilled. In 1878, William E. Blackstone, a self-educated farm boy from Adams, New York, wrote a best-selling book, *Jesus Is Coming,* which set forth Blackstone's Zionist ideas about the end times. Blackstone traveled to the Holy Land, met the young Jewish pioneers, and declared them to be living proof that God was right on time.

In 1891, in the midst of a wave of Russian pogroms, Blackstone circulated a petition titled "What shall be done for the Russian Jews?" "Why not give Palestine back to them again?" he demanded. "According to God's distribution of nations, it is their home—an inalienable possession from which they were expelled by force. . . .

"A million exiles, by their terrible sufferings, are piteously appealing to our sympathy, justice and humanity. Let us now restore them to the land of which they were cruelly despoiled by our Roman ancestors."

Blackstone's petition was signed by 413 leading Americans— virtually all of them Christians—including Melville Fuller, Chief Justice of the United States Supreme Court; Thomas Reed, Speaker of the House of Representatives; John D. Rockefeller,

Cyrus McCormick, and J. P. Morgan. Blackstone, who by this time was calling himself "God's little errand boy," sent it to President Benjamin Harrison, who proceeded to ignore it.

In 1916, Blackstone tried again. This time the signatories were lesser figures, but the president, Woodrow Wilson, was more sympathetic. The following year, on the eve of the British conquest of Palestine, when British foreign minister Arthur Balfour, himself a devout Protestant, promised a Jewish national home, Wilson said amen.

Blackstone and his fellow American evangelicals saw World War I and the Balfour Declaration as further signs of biblical prophecy. By the end of the war, kibbutzim had been established in the Galilee and the Sharon Plain; the first Jewish city, Tel Aviv, was founded on the sands of the Mediterranean; and the Jewish population of Palestine reached 80,000. "Prophetic conferences" were held in churches throughout the United States, and developments in the Holy Land were checked against biblical predictions. The prospect of a Jewish state in Zion was more exciting to American Christians than to American Jews.

ISRAEL AFTER THE Holocaust should have been an easy sell in the United States, but it wasn't. The Truman administration grudgingly recognized the Jewish state but slapped an arms embargo on it in 1948, during Israel's War of Independence. Six thousand Israeli soldiers died in that war—roughly 1 percent of the entire Jewish population of Palestine—while the United States withheld military support and the FBI chased down Zionist-American gunrunners.

The State Department was strongly opposed to the creation of Israel (a hostility that persisted for decades). The American foreign policy establishment tended to what is now called "realism," which placed a higher value on Arab oil producers than on Israel. In the 1956 Suez War, President Eisenhower directly threatened Israeli prime minister David Ben-Gurion with severe sanctions and forced him to make a humiliating withdrawal from the conquered Sinai Peninsula. Although a lot of American Jews had voted for Ike, he refused to even meet with a delegation of Jewish pro-Israel lobbyists.

The Kennedy administration was friendlier, but not much. Jews hated Nixon so much that they were able to forgive JFK for his father's pro-Hitler stance before World War II. But Kennedy kept Israel at arm's length, giving it little financial aid or diplomatic cover, and even refusing to host a state visit for Prime Minister David Ben-Gurion, flying up to New York City to meet him informally instead. Not until Lyndon Johnson's administration was an Israeli leader, Levi Eshkol, officially received at the White House. Johnson saw Israel as an important ally as well as a kindred pioneer democracy, an attitude that was strengthened by Israeli military success in the Six-Day War.

It was the hated Nixon who first made Israel a foreign aid priority and sold it large quantities of advanced American weapons. Like Johnson, Nixon regarded Israel as a regional power worth cultivating. He also had hopes of detaching Jewish voters from the Democratic coalition (an ambition that he partially, if temporarily, fulfilled in the 1972 election, with an assist from his opponent, George McGovern). During these years, the organized evangelical Christian community did not play a serious role in foreign policy (or domestic politics, for that matter). When evangelical interest did venture beyond U.S. borders, it generally focused on missionary work. But even in its most politically passive period, the prophetic understanding of history, and the place of Israel in it, remained a central factor in evangelical theological thinking. In 1961, the Zionist lyric of the theme song to the movie *Exodus* ("This land is mine, God gave this land to me") was written not by one of the legion of Jewish songwriters in the Brill Building, but by the born-again Christian crooner Pat Boone.

At the time, American Jews didn't know or care what Pat Boone believed God was up to. In the sixties, they and their Christian liberal role models saw evangelicals as Holy Rollers, snake oil salesmen, or KKK night riders, the sort of backward goyim portrayed in films like *Elmer Gantry* and *Inherit the Wind.* Postwar Jewry was big on "interfaith": marching with Martin Luther King Jr., working with ethnic Catholics in big-city Democratic clubhouses, or attending brotherhood hootenannies in the basement of the local Episcopal church. It most certainly didn't approve of cooperating with people who thought that Satan was real, Jesus was coming any day, and angels watched over the world.

IN JULY 2006, there were a lot of angel people in Denver. They were in town for the International Christian Retail Show, a born-again extravaganza that brings together wholesalers, retailers, and curious customers for an annual orgy of Christian commerce. The show was held in the Denver Convention Center, and I shared a cab there from my hotel with an evangelical Hollywood producer who was desperately seeking tall actors. She was making a film about a miracle that supposedly took place at the World Trade Center during 9/11, she told me, and she needed seven-footers.

"Why do they have to be so tall?" I asked.

"Because they'll be playing angels."

"Are angels tall?"

The producer had evidently assumed that I was the sort of guy who knew something about angels. Now disabused, she said,

"Children who see angels describe them as over seven feet high. With wings."

"I've heard that, about the wings," I said.

Angels were a big item at the Christian Retail Show. There were angel books, angel videocassettes, angel candle pots on display. A company called Ken Enterprises LLC offered an entire catalog of angel paraphernalia. But angels were just the start of what was available. Thousands of vendors offered every imaginable sort of Jesus gear, from medical "scripture scrubs" adorned with prayers (not the most reassuring thing, I would imagine, for a patient in need of emergency treatment) to evangelical high fashion from Divinity Boutique. Still, there was a fair amount of diversity. The menu in the main cafeteria offered kosher Hebrew National hot dogs, and at the entrance to the convention center there was a poster advertising an upcoming exhibit featuring "flesh-eating dinosaurs," which didn't seem to bother any of the creationists in the crowd.

There were thousands of books, videos, and compact discs on sale: salvation through communication. My eye was caught by a booth draped in Israeli flags.

Boxes of a videocassette, *Israel, Islam and Armageddon: The Final Battle for Jerusalem,* were stacked on a counter next to a laminated letter of endorsement from an Israeli general I had never heard of. A young salesman came over to me and said, "This is a great Israeli war hero and he fully supports Dave Hunt's ministry."

The salesman pointed to a large framed photograph of Dave Hunt, an elderly chap with a white beard. He looked slightly wild-eyed and unkempt, the sort of man you might see eating dinner alone in a diner on a national holiday.

"Would you like to meet Reverend Hunt himself?" the salesman offered. Before I could answer, Reverend Hunt was upon me. He had a keen expression and held a banana in his hand. Skipping the introductions, he said, "Do you know how many times the Bible refers to God as God of Israel?"

"Ah, no."

"Two hundred and three times! That's two hundred and three."

I emitted a low whistle.

"Do you know how many times God is called the God of Abraham, Isaac, and Jacob?" he demanded. "In the Bible? Twelve times! That's twelve." Hunt took a healthy bite of his banana. "And do you know how many times the Bible refers to God as the God of Islam?" He punctuated the question with a hard swallow.

"None?"

"Exactly correct!" said Hunt. "None. Come to my lecture this afternoon. I'm going to be discussing this in detail."

"I'll probably be there," I said, guiltily; I hated to lie to a man of the cloth. But this evidently satisfied Hunt. "Remember, two hundred and three times," he called after me as I walked away. I looked back and saw he was waving his empty banana peel at me. "Two hundred and three times versus *none.*"

As I wandered among the booths, I noticed a smattering of blacks, a few Catholic priests and nuns, and an occasional Jewish vendor peddling Holy Land goods ("Most of this *schlock* is made in China," one confided to me in Hebrew). But, by and large, the crowd was white, Protestant, conservative, and Republican. Tapes and books extolling George W. Bush were prominent. Red, white, and blue bunting hung from the walls. The entire scene exuded a sense of Christian capitalist energy and optimism, a gathering of merchants with God knows how many customers, and more saved every day.

I was aware that I stood out, but I felt welcome. Vendors, after scrutinizing my name tag, called out "Shalom." An elderly woman told me she spends part of every year in the Galilee praying for the Jews and demanded to know if I do the same. A tall, reedy fellow who reminded me of Homer Simpson's friend Flanders shook my hand. "You an Israeli?" he asked in a hickory-flavored Tennessee Hebrew he had acquired during a year on a kibbutz. "I *love* Israelis."

AMONG THE COMPANIES represented at the Denver Convention Center was the Barna Group, a West Coast firm that specializes in studying and analyzing the evangelical community. It had just completed a survey of born-again Christians that provides what is probably the best baseline for understanding who evangelicals are and what they believe.

The survey began by assessing the overall number of born-again Christians based on two essential criteria: people who had "made a personal commitment to Jesus Christ that was still important in their lives today" and who believe that when they die they will go to heaven "because they had confessed their sins and accepted Jesus Christ as their savior." Roughly 40 percent of Americans—about 120 million people—fall into this category.

Barna then set up seven criteria intended to separate the evangelical lite from the hard stuff:

1. Is faith very important in your daily life?

2. Do you feel a personal responsibility to share your belief with non-Christians?

3. Do you believe in the existence of Satan?

4. Do you hold that personal salvation is possible only through faith, not works?

5. Do you assert that Jesus led a sinless life on Earth?

6. Do you believe that the Bible is totally accurate in all it teaches?

7. Would you describe God as the "all-knowing, all powerful perfect deity who created the universe and still rules it today"?

Barna found that 7 percent of Americans—more than 20 million people—fit this more stringent set of criteria. These are the people who form the core of the Christian Zionist movement.

Many Jews believe that the real motive of evangelical support for Israel is criterion number two: the desire to share their belief in Jesus with others, especially with Jews. But in fact it is the sixth criterion—a literal belief in the Bible—that is most crucial. The Bible, as it is read by hard-core evangelicals, is a Zionist document that clearly states God's covenant with the people of Israel. The Jews have been chosen, whether it seems like a good choice or not. They are the apple of God's eye. Israel is promised to them. Period.

Liberal American Jews are intensely uncomfortable with this formulation. It's not that they disagree with the notion of Jewish superiority—*New York* magazine ran a cover story in October 2005 whose title, "Are Jews Smarter?" was widely seen in the Jewish community as a rhetorical question. But liberal Jews do not take the Bible literally. They certainly don't accept the New Testament as scripture. And they most especially disagree with the notion that the Jews have a unique role in the End of Days.

This idea is not universally believed in the evangelical community, either. And it is far from the only reason conservative Christians support Israel. In 2002, the International Fellowship of Christians and Jews, an organization founded by Rabbi Yechiel

Eckstein, conducted a poll that found that, "contrary to conventional wisdom, a minority of evangelicals cite theological belief as the reason why they support Israel."

"Israelis cried with us when we were attacked and the towers fell," I was told by former GOP presidential candidate Gary Bauer, a consultant to the IFCJ. "When we look at the world, we have a tendency to identify Israel as the good guys." Bauer dismissed those who believe in Armageddon and the death of the Jews as marginal, "just a few people with odd beliefs."

This understates the case. It's true that, in the IFCJ survey, a plurality of Israel's conservative Christian supporters say they are primarily moved by secular, geopolitical considerations. But it is also true that 35 percent mentioned eschatological belief as their main motivation.

These are the audience for the Left Behind series of Tim LaHaye and Jerry B. Jenkins, a dozen books about the End of Days that have collectively sold more than 65 million copies.

THE NOVELS, PUBLISHED by Tyndale, a Christian company in Wheaton, Illinois, are a science fiction version of the book of Revelation. One day, so the story goes, millions of saved Christians suddenly disappear from Earth, "raptured" up to the sky by God. Widespread panic ensues. The world, searching for leadership, reaches out to Nicolae Jetty Carpathia, a dashing young former president of Romania, now secretary-general of the UN, who preaches peace to camouflage his goal of Satanic domination. For the first three and a half years of his reign he is widely perceived as a benevolent dictator. Then he reveals himself to be the Antichrist. The resistance is led by the Tribulation Force, a group of unsaved people (Jews as well as nominal Christians) who have been left behind and now see the light. Battles follow on the road to the final showdown, at Armageddon. When the series ends, Carpathia will be defeated and Christ will rule in Jerusalem for a thousand years.

Vast numbers of Christians believe variations of this story. Many think it will take place in their lifetime. A few are already in the Holy Land, awaiting the End of Days. Bill and Connie Wilson are two of these people.

THREE

THE GROCERY STORE AT THE END OF THE WORLD

I met the Wilsons on a steaming August morning in Tel Aviv. They picked me up at my house in a Volvo jalopy with a busted air conditioner. Our destination was Armageddon.

The Wilsons are ordained Pentecostal preachers, middle-aged folks on their second marriage. Bill is a friendly, round-faced man with an engineering degree from Georgia Tech; he is also a retired brigadier general in the Georgia National Guard. A self-proclaimed square, he signed a temperance pledge when he was eleven years old and stubbornly honored it until he started coming to Israel a few years ago. "You go to somebody's house for Shabbat dinner, you naturally take a sip or two of kiddush wine," he drawled.

Connie is an attractive, outgoing woman who came to Christianity after what she describes as a pagan lifestyle. "I channeled the seventies," she says. When she found Christ, she fell hard, becoming a disciple of revivalist Ruth Ward Heflin, a peripatetic preacher known for holding camp meetings where, according to *Charisma Magazine,* people claimed that gold dust appeared on their faces and hands and rubies replaced their dental fillings.

When Pastor Heflin died in 2000, the Wilsons inherited her Mount Zion Fellowship ministry in Jerusalem.

The drive from Tel Aviv to Armageddon took a little more than an hour, up the coastal road along the Mediterranean and then eastward into the Jezreel Valley. To Israelis, this is the agricultural heartland of the Galilee, an area dotted with red-roofed villages and collective farms. To Bill and Connie it is *terra sancta.*

Just the day before, the Israeli army had begun evacuating Jewish settlers from the Gaza Strip. The withdrawal was still going on, and the Wilsons saw it as the first step in an eventual Israeli departure from Judea and Samaria. This prospect dismayed them; giving biblical land to Muslims seemed a step in the wrong direction. But they weren't inclined to be hard on Prime Minister Ariel Sharon. Like many evangelicals, they had the ability to compartmentalize. Sharon was the elected leader of a democratic ally. In the short term, he would do what he considered best and they would support him. As for the long run, well, that wasn't up to Sharon or to them. God would unfold his plan in his own time.

"This is the place," Bill announced, turning onto a one-lane country road. Up ahead was a sign that read "Kibbutz Megiddo/ Tel Megiddo National Park." The kibbutz was founded in the 1940s by Holocaust survivors who were very likely unaware of the place's Christian eschatological significance. They did know, however, that it was the site of an ancient city. An archaeological excavation got under way and buses of schoolkids occasionally stopped to view the dig and eat lunch in a small café. But Kibbutz Meggido was a sleepy little community until the 1980s when the evangelicals began visiting.

Megiddo became a destination. An impressive store specializing in Roman glass jewelry and biblical-style artifacts opened up. The café was expanded. For the first time in millennia, Har

Megiddo, which the Christians translate as "Armageddon," was on the map.

"IT'S HARD TO imagine this whole peaceful valley in a blood-bath," said Connie Wilson. We were standing on the top of a hill overlooking the Jezreel Valley, in a spot she imagined to be ground zero.

Bill cast a Georgia guardsman's eye over the terrain. "I suppose there will be tanks, helicopters, artillery all used in concert, coming from that direction," he said, pointing northeast. "I don't know what our forces would do about cover and concealment—there isn't much down there, just a plain. Maybe they'd position themselves in the hills on the other side of the Jordan River and wait for the enemy to make a stupid mistake."

For an army commanded by God, this struck me as a rather pedestrian plan of battle, and I said so. Bill shrugged. "Maybe it will go nuclear," he said. "Wipe out the enemy that way. Don't forget, the enemy forces are going to number about two hundred million troops."

"I doubt that this valley can hold that many people," I said. "The entire population of Israel is only six million and already you can't find a parking spot."

Bill didn't crack a smile. "This is the place that God has prepared and chosen for his plan, according to the Bible. He'll bring Israel's enemies right here and then he'll say, 'The Jews are my people and enough is enough!' That's when he'll go into action."

"Imagine the Twin Towers times, oh, I don't know how many," said Connie. "It will take seven years just to clean the blood and bodies after the battle." She wasn't preaching or trying to convince me; she was describing a certainty.

A young woman journalist had accompanied us that day, and Connie turned to her. "You live in Israel, right? You consider yourself an Israeli. But where were you born?"

"Argentina," said the journalist.

"And you come from the United States," she said to me. "So listen to this." She opened her Bible and began reading from Jeremiah. "'Behold, I will gather them out of all the countries whither I have driven them, in mine anger, and in my fury, and in great wrath; and I will bring them again unto this place, and I will cause them to dwell safely.' That's God talking about the ingathering of the Jews from around the world into the state of Israel.

"And it's there in Ezekiel, too. 'And he said unto me, Son of man, these bones are the whole house of Israel. Behold, they say, Our bones are dried, and our hope is lost: we are cut off! Therefore prophesy and say unto them, Thus saith the Lord Jehovah: Behold, I will open your graves, and cause you to come up out of your graves, O my people, and bring you into the land of Israel.'"

THE EARLY ZIONISTS knew these Bible stories too; they learned them in the dank Hebrew schools of Poland and Russia and the Austro-Hungarian Empire. The Bible was full of promises of national restoration, but the promises were two thousand years old and the pioneers were young and impatient.

They wanted a revolution, so they created one.

Some of the more assimilated Western Jewish Zionists, like Theodor Herzl, the founder of the modern Zionist movement, had been willing to consider a Jewish state in Uganda or South America. But proposals to decouple Zionism from Zion didn't fly with the Jewish masses, so the secular nationalists made a virtue of the Bible they didn't believe in, turning it into a recruiting tool, a nation-building myth, and—when they discovered evangelical

Christians in the British Foreign Office—an argument for a Jewish national home in Palestine.

Soon enough, the biblical seducers seduced themselves. How could it be otherwise? Bible-sized events were taking place all around them. "To be a realist here, you have to believe in miracles," David Ben-Gurion once remarked. He didn't believe that literally, of course; he was an atheist. But he insisted that his officials and generals take Old Testament names. He compared his favorite military man, Moshe Dayan, to the biblical conqueror Joshua Bin-Nun, which flattered them both. After all, Joshua worked for Moses.

In 1971, Ben-Gurion, out of office but still a national icon, greeted a conference of fifteen hundred evangelical Christians in Jerusalem. It was a gala event, held in the recently opened national convention center. Never before had there been such a gathering of Christian Zionists in the Holy Land. Anita Bryant, the former Miss Oklahoma, sang the Israeli national anthem. Carl Henry, the editor of *Christianity Today*, and other luminaries of the American evangelical community preached. Their theme was that the Six-Day War, which had put Jerusalem back in Jewish hands for the first time in two millennia, was a sure sign that the Second Coming of Jesus was on the way.

Ben-Gurion himself was ambivalent about the results of the Six-Day War (particularly since he had been excluded from wartime leadership—and the reflected glory of victory—by his rival and successor, Levi Eshkol). But he couldn't miss its potential for arousing support for Israel among Christians. Something was in the air.

The United States was being swept by a strange new book full of Christian Zionist predictions, *The Late Great Planet Earth*, by Hal Lindsey. "Nations would fit into a certain power pattern [based on] the most important sign of all—that is the Jew returning to the Land of Israel after thousands of years of being dispersed," Lindsey wrote. "The Jew is the most important sign to this generation." When Ben-Gurion died in 1973, Lindsey's book was on a reading table in his cottage at Kibbutz Sde Boker.

BILL AND CONNIE Wilson are Lindsey fans. They see the pattern. The book of Ezekiel says that Israel will be attacked from the "uttermost parts of the north." They take this, according to their reading of the Bible, as a reference to Russia, in league with Persia (Iran), Ethiopia, some other African countries (Egypt, Sudan), and China.

As if this weren't enough, they think the Roman Empire is about to make a comeback. ("Remind you of the European Union?" asked Bill). It will be led by a smooth trickster. Connie read from the book of Revelation: "'And it deceives those that dwell upon the earth by reason of the signs which it was given to it to work before the beast, saying to those that dwell upon the earth to make an image to the beast, which has the wound of the sword, and lived.'"

The beast, Connie explained, is the Antichrist, who gets his power through the dragon. The book of Revelation tells you who that is: "'And the great dragon was cast out, the ancient serpent, he who is called Devil and Satan.'"

After the great battle, Connie said, the dragon would be defeated, Jesus would reign in Jerusalem, and the whole world would know and worship God.

"If God can do anything, why not just do it without all these beasts and devils and so forth?" I asked.

"He wants to send a message to humanity," said Connie. "This is his plan. That's how he has prepared it." She sounded as certain as a climate scientist describing global warming. But, like apocalyptic climate scenarios, Armageddon is longer on prediction than actual data. Revelation is full of obscure symbolism; there's plenty of room for creativity. Not everyone, for example, believes that saved Christians will be raptured up to the sky before the beginning of the seven-year tribulation. Some, like Pat Robertson, hold that the rapture will occur only after the tribulation, and that during it saved Christians will suffer right along with everyone else. There is also dispute over the identity of the Antichrist. Premillennialists have traditionally suspected that he will be the pope, and a few still do. During World War II, it was widely held among evangelicals that the Antichrist was Hitler, and during the cold war, Stalin. Lately Osama Bin Laden has developed a following. Revelation is nothing if not open to interpretation.

Evangelical Christians have long debated these nuances but their eschatology was of no interest to the outside world until born-agains became politically potent. Suddenly there was great liberal suspicion that George W Bush, with his "evildoers" and his inexplicable love of Israel, was unduly influenced by the Bible. At the start of the American invasion of Iraq, a BBC correspondent in Washington spoke for many in the international press corps when he asked, rhetorically, "Does the president believe that he is playing a part in the final events of Armageddon?" Similar concerns were raised twenty years earlier about Ronald Reagan.

Evangelical Christians, however, do not believe that they are called upon to play a role in making Armageddon come to pass. That's God's job. Nor does an American president have to be a born-again Christian to contemplate blowing up the world. The framers of the cold war policy of mutually assured destruction (MAD) weren't religious fanatics. John F. Kennedy, who was prepared to start a nuclear war with the Soviet Union over missiles in Cuba, was not known for his piety. Richard Nixon, a nominal

Quaker, put the United States on high nuclear alert during the 1973 Yom Kippur War. In the atomic age, Armageddon can come in a lot of forms.

JEWISH LIBERALS TEND to get very upset about the part they are assigned in evangelical eschatology. "The Jews die or convert," says Gershom Gorenberg, author of the book *End of Days: Fundamentalism and the Struggle for the Temple Mount.* "As a Jew, I can't feel very comfortable with the affections of somebody who looks forward to that scenario."

Gorenberg is a fine writer and a former colleague at the *Jerusalem Report,* but it is unclear to me why he needs to feel "comfortable" with beliefs he considers fanciful in the first place. Either the evangelicals are right or they are wrong about the end times. If they are wrong, what difference does it make? And if it turns out they are right, Gorenberg and I and the rest of the Jews will have some 'splainin' to do to Jesus.

STANDING IN THE sun at Armageddon thinking about the end times is thirsty business. I suggested to the Wilsons that we get a cold drink in a nearby town—a little place called Omen. We piled in the Volvo and headed up the road a mile or two.

"My goodness," said Connie, looking at the sign as we turned into a village. "I've never noticed *this* place before. Omen!"

"He works in strange ways," I said. Actually *omen* in Hebrew doesn't have anything to do with the English word "omen," but I let that stay my little secret. The Antichrist isn't the only trickster on the block.

Omen's grocery is a cramped little store run by a jovial, mustachioed fellow named Motti. He doesn't get a lot of strangers dropping in, and he greeted us with delighted hospitality. A small TV over the checkout counter was broadcasting scenes of the evacuation of Israeli settlers from the Gaza Strip.

"Those poor soldiers," said a young woman standing next to the cash register. She wore the uniform of the artillery corps. It's illegal for soldiers to work civilian jobs; I figured she might be an off-duty relative of Motti's. "All that equipment they're wearing and the helmets. It's so hot down there."

"You've got to be crazy to live in Gaza," said a young guy in jeans who was lounging nearby, smoking a Marlboro.

"Look who's talking," I said. "You live five minutes from the End of the World."

The guy smiled in rueful agreement. "End of the world" in Hebrew means "the middle of nowhere."

"Literally," I said. I nodded toward the Wilsons who were drinking Cokes and staring at the live feed from Gaza. "They think the world is going to come to an end at Megiddo, in a huge battle."

"*Mah attah omer?*" he said, the Hebrew equivalent of "Say what?"

"It's a Christian belief."

"Ah, Christians," said the young Israeli dismissively.

"Did you say at Megiddo?" said the cashier. "The kibbutz?" She appeared to be mentally calibrating the distance, which was only a couple of miles. "My boyfriend lives on that kibbutz."

"Don't worry about it," Motti said. "People believe whatever they want to believe."

The door opened and in walked three women, dressed in simple gray cloth dresses that reached the ground. Two were young—one was pregnant—and the third appeared to be in her sixties. Their skin was the color of parchment and their eyes were narrow almonds. They stood in the entrance to the store speechless, looking utterly lost.

"Bnai Menashe," Motti said to me. "They just got here last night from Gaza."

Bnai Menashe—purportedly the lost tribe of Manasseh—had recently been discovered in the wilds of northern India along the Burmese border. Most were still in their villages, waiting to be brought to Israel. But some were already here.

"Good afternoon," I greeted the women in Hebrew. "Do any of you speak English?"

One of the younger women murmured "Hebrew," in a way that made it clear she didn't know any.

I turned to Motti. "Why were they sent here, to Omen of all places?"

Motti turned his palms up; he had no idea. "They'll be all right here, though," he said. "It's a friendly place. We all started out as immigrants. Russians, Tunisians, we all get along."

The women turned up an aisle and began looking at a display of eggs. Motti went over to help.

As FAR AS is known, the Bnai Menashe come from a people who were Christianized by Protestant missionaries in the nineteenth century. From there it was apparently a short jump to imagining themselves to be lost Hebrews. Once they started calling themselves Israelites, rumors reached Jerusalem. Rabbis who specialize in tracing vestigial Jews began showing up in their villages. Money was donated, synagogues formed, Hebrew taught, prayers introduced. Soon some of the Bnai Menashe wanted to go to Israel.

The Jewish farmers of the Gaza Strip had been short of Arab agricultural workers since the first intifada in the late 1980s. They liked the idea of cheap Jewish labor, even if it came from a biblical tribe. Right-wing Israeli politicians, concerned about the demographic balance between Jews and Arabs, got behind the idea too. Eventually the Israeli Chief Rabbinate declared that, although these tribesmen weren't Jews, they were Jew*ish,* eligible for expedited conversion, which under Israel's Law of Return meant repatriation to the land of their fathers with full immigrant housing, medical, and educational benefits. A biblical tribe was born.

In the times of the Bible, the tribe of Manasseh is said to have inhabited the very area where Omen is located. I mentioned this to the soldier-cashier, but she gave me a blank look and said, "Hey, I saw them yesterday for the first time."

Connie Wilson took pictures of the women to document her brush with the book of Ezekiel. Here were her dried bones made flesh and standing in the poultry aisle. Motti helped them sort through the eggs, placing them gingerly, one at a time, into the wire shopping basket. "Do you believe they're really part of a lost tribe?" I asked him.

Motti smiled. "If they think they are, then they are," he replied. "Why argue about it?" In the grocery store at the End of the World the customer is always right.

FOUR

CELL PHONE CONVERSION

Let me ask you a personal question," the woman said in a flat Michigan accent. "Have you accepted Jesus Christ as your savior?"

There was a long pause on the other end of the line.

Finally I said, "Ah, no," to the woman, whose name was Sue Ricksecker. She is the secretary of Emmanuel Baptist in Pontiac, the site of my teenage brush with Jesus. I had called to find out if, by any chance, the church files still contained the little personal information card I had filled out forty years ago (under the name of Rabbi Ernst Conrad) at the Hyman Appleman revival. But that moment evidently doesn't loom as large in the institutional memory of Emmanuel Baptist as it does in mine. In any event, there was no record of it.

I thanked Sue for checking. "You're very welcome," she said. And then she asked me her personal question, about accepting Jesus.

"I'm Jewish," I said, by way of explanation. This had been my mother's standard answer to Mormon door-to-door missionaries when I was a kid. They always seemed to accept it without argument, at which point she would invite them in for lemonade and raptly watch their documentary films about how Jesus was really from upstate New York.

Sue was made of sterner stuff. "There are a lot of Jewish Christians," she said reasonably. "Dr. Hyman Appleman was Jewish. *Jesus* was Jewish."

"Yeah, but was he a Christian?"

"He was *Christ*," she said. Humor isn't necessarily the best way to communicate with church secretaries. "Can I ask you one more personal question? What would happen if you died right now? I mean right this second, if you had a heart attack and keeled right over and died."

That's exactly the way my father died, but Sue had no way of knowing that. Did she? "I don't know what would happen," I said. "When you're dead you're dead."

"You'd go to hell," said Sue sweetly. "Seriously. You. Would. Go. To. Hell. That's not me telling you, me Sue, that's what it says in the Bible."

"Ah, okay. So thanks for your time and . . ."

"Wait! Let me ask just one more personal question. What would happen if you *accepted* Jesus? I mean right now, here on the phone, with me. And then you died? You'd go right to heaven. And do you know the first thing you'd see when you opened your eyes?"

"What?"

"The first thing you'd see when you opened your eyes would be Jesus' smiling face."

"Do you know the second thing I'd see after I opened my eyes?" I asked.

"No. What?"

"I'd see my grandfather with a Louisville slugger in his hand."

"I'm sure your grandfather would be very happy for you," she said solemnly, although how a socialist Jew like my grandfather would have gotten to heaven in the first place is a mystery she didn't tackle. "Just open your heart, accept Jesus, and you'll be saved for eternity."

"Simple as that."

"Simple as that."

"Aw, I can't do it," I said. "Really, I appreciate the offer, but no thanks."

"I'm going to be praying that you change your mind," she said.

"Go ahead."

"Praying for you every day of my life."

"That's really nice of you."

"I mean it. I want you to call me when you accept Jesus. I want to witness it. I can do that right on the phone. I've done it for others. Will you call me?"

"Sure," I said, but I had my fingers crossed.

"I'm going to give you a number," she said. "Please write it down."

"What kind of number?"

"My cell phone. I want you to call me when you change your heart," she said. "And in the meantime I'll be praying for your salvation from now every day for the rest of my life."

Later, when I told this story to Lisa, she shrugged.

"Now you know what it's like to be a woman."

"Meaning?"

"Getting hit on."

"It's kind of flattering in a way."

"She's an evangelical," Lisa said. "She hits on everyone."

THE NOTION THAT evangelicals are only being friendly in order to convert the Jews to Christ is second only to alarms over Armageddon in the dark imaginings of Jews. And there is a certain amount of truth to it. Evangelicals want to evangelize. And, unlike the Second Coming, winning souls isn't something you wait around for Jesus to take care of. You're supposed to do it yourself.

In 1996, the Southern Baptist Convention, the largest evangelical denomination, called on its members to direct their "energies and resources toward the proclamation of the gospel to the Jewish people." Three years later, the International Mission Board suggested that missionaries step up their work during Rosh Hashanah and Yom Kippur on the (very dubious) grounds that during the High Holidays Jews are in a great state of spiritual receptivity. More recently, the SBC has been considering using messianic Jews—such as the much-despised Jews for Jesus—as missionaries.

The American Jewish community faces problems, but mass conversion to evangelical Christianity isn't one of them. The community has been shrinking for fifty years—from about 6 million after World War II to something closer to 5 million today—despite large immigrations from Russia, Iran, South America, and Israel. But very few of the lost sheep have wandered into the evangelical flock. Secular Jews marry late and have small families. Nowadays, at least half marry non-Jews. What Jews *don't* do is get born again. There are probably more ex-Jewish Buddhists than Baptists in the United States.

THE EVANGELICAL EFFORT to convert the Jews has a long history of failure in the United States. Around the turn of the twentieth century, evangelicals began setting up missions to the Jewish immigrants in the big cities. The indefatigable William E. Blackstone himself created the Chicago Committee for Hebrew Christian Work. In New York, evangelists like Arno Gaebelein, a German Lutheran who preached in Yiddish, and Herman Warsza-

wiak, who supposedly recruited his audience by handing out free
movie tickets, set up operations that met with very little success.
Many Orthodox Jews regarded these missionaries (and all Christians) with loathing; the very pious among them held card parties
on Christmas Eve to demonstrate their contempt. The socialists,
communists, anarchists, and free-thinkers among the Jewish intelligentsia hated all religion. Meanwhile, the grassroots majority
were too busy trying to make a living to involve themselves in
theological debates. Community elders complained about the as-
similative power of the new country but the expression *America
gonif* ("America, the thief") referred to the lures of secular
culture—the English language, baseball, and the pork chop—not
Christianity.

None of this kept the evangelicals from hoping. In 1923, the
Moody Bible Institute in Chicago set up the first chair in Jewish
Studies and hired a converted Jewish professor to teach the art
and science of capturing Jews for Christ. The New Testament was
translated into Yiddish (don't ask how *that* sounded). But for the
most part it was wasted effort. The Jews who did convert were
most often second- and third-generation, upper-class Germans
with social aspirations. The Sulzbergers, Pulitzers, Warburgs, and
Strausses who crossed the line wound up in Episcopal cathedrals
or Unitarian meeting halls, not Baptist revival tents.

In 1964, the American Board of Missions to the Jews (ABMJ)—
a Brooklyn Christian outreach founded by a converted Hungar-
ian rabbi, Leopold Cohn, at the end of the nineteenth
century—set up a booth at the New York World's Fair that was
widely ignored. Seven years later, the same group ran a full-page
ad in the *New York Times. This* caused a ripple because it coincided
with the emergence of a new movement, Jews for Jesus.

Jews for Jesus was the creation of an ABMJ missionary, Moishe
Rosen. Born in 1931 and raised a secular Jew, he found Jesus in

Denver (the same place Hyman Appleman was converted a generation earlier). Rosen had a good eye for the sort of words and music that would appeal to young Americans in the Age of Aquarius. He also understood the Jewish taboo against conversion. So he took a novel approach: he taught that becoming a Christian didn't make you a goy. "Please don't call me a converted Jew!" Rosen wrote. "I was born a Jew and I'll die a Jew. . . . I am pleased to be a Jew and part of a noble people who have brought so much to the rest of the world." You could do your own thing, be a Jew *and* a Christian—just like Jesus, whom Rosen called Y'shua.

Jews for Jesus became the best known of a number of messianic Jewish movements and congregations (Rosen himself spun off from the ABMJ board in 1973 and set up an independent group). They formed their own congregations and created their own rituals and lingo. Perhaps the high point of the Jews for Jesus movement was Bob Dylan's "Christian period" in the late 1970s and early 1980s, when he recorded three religious albums, and Norman Greenbaum's hit song "Spirit in the Sky" ("Gotta have a friend in Jesus"), which became a born-again anthem. Still, Greenbaum never converted and Dylan eventually came wandering home.

Today, evangelical outreach to the Jews is most likely to come via bad TV. Televangelists like Reverend Sid Roth have all the charisma of certified public accountants, while messianic infomercials intersperse the hawking of Jewish ritual merchandise with scenes of unattractive people dancing the hora. All this enforces a message to American Jews: evangelical Christianity is a major step down the social ladder.

Of course, there are Jews who *have* become born-again Christians, and a few have leadership roles in the evangelical world.

Marvin Olasky, a professor at the University of Texas, coined the term "compassionate conservative" and has been a spiritual and intellectual influence on George W Bush. Jay Sekulow runs Pat Robertson's American Center for Law and Justice, the born-again equivalent of the ACLU; he was named one of the country's twenty-five most influential evangelicals by *Time* magazine. Joel Rosenberg, a best-selling writer of End of Days fiction, describes himself as "a nice Jewish-Christian boy from Syracuse." But, with apologies to these luminaries, they represent a pretty thin harvest for a hundred-year missionary effort.

ONE OF THE great differences between evangelical Christianity and Judaism is that Jews don't proselytize. Orthodox rabbis are enjoined to discourage potential converts three times, and some of them are very good at it. If they *do* take you on, there are no cell phone conversions. You get a makeover—new diet, clothes, neighborhood (walking distance to a synagogue), even a new name. And in Israel, where the Orthodox rabbis have a monopoly on conversion, sometimes even becoming a Jew isn't enough to make you Jewish, as my friend Viktor found out when they put him in jail.

Viktor is a tall, blue-eyed, blond-haired, soft-spoken young fellow who grew up in a Romanian farm village near the Serbian border. One day, while visiting Bucharest, he met a tourist from Tel Aviv. She and Viktor fell in love, he got an Israeli visa, and they returned together to Israel.

The young woman was not in any way religious. Neither were her parents. But they wanted a wedding in Israel, where there are no mixed marriages. Viktor would need to convert to Judaism. So Viktor set out in search of a rabbi.

But everywhere he went he got the runaround. As far as the rabbis of Israel were concerned there were already too many tall, blue-eyed Russian immigrant gentiles running around, and if a Romanian wasn't exactly a Russian, what was the difference?

For months Viktor searched, until he finally found a small, off-brand ultra-Orthodox yeshiva in Jerusalem that was ready to take him on. It belonged to a minor opposition political party—religious institutions in Israel support political parties and are financed by the government—but Viktor wasn't alive to, or interested in, such partisan nuances.

If the rabbis suspected that Viktor was merely a convert of convenience, they were mistaken. He quickly decided that he was a devout Jew trapped in a gentile's body. He began dressing like a Forty-seventh Street diamond dealer, complete with black suit and hat, ritual prayer fringes peeking out from under his white shirt. He started speaking Hebrew laced with Yiddish expressions and Talmudic aphorisms. It didn't take him long to decide that it was wrong for him to be shacked up out of wedlock, so he and his girlfriend broke up.

In Romania, Viktor had been a massage therapist and he maintained a small practice in Jerusalem. Giving rubdowns wasn't exactly an approved activity for yeshiva boys, but Viktor wasn't a standard student, and besides, he kicked back a portion of his income to the yeshiva.

This lucrative arrangement may have accounted for Viktor's relatively slow progress. After a number of years, though, it was no longer feasible to keep turning him down. His final test was living for an entire year under the supervision of an ultra-Orthodox family. At the end of this trial period he was circumcised, dipped in the ritual bath, and pronounced Jewish.

Certificate of conversion in hand, Viktor headed for the Ministry of the Interior. He thought he was covered by the Law of Return, which grants automatic Israeli citizenship to any Jew, converted or otherwise, who applied for it. As soon as he got his papers, he intended to hire a matchmaker, find a kosher bride, and settle in Jerusalem, a Jew in good standing.

The Ministry of Interior turned down Viktor's conversion, ostensibly because it had been granted by ultra-Orthodox rabbis instead of state-employed rabbinical officials. Viktor, who had grown savvy over the years, suspected that the real reason was that the new minister of the interior was a member of the anticlerical party Shinui and wanted to give black-hat rabbis a hard time. Either way, Viktor was screwed. The ministry not only turned down his application for citizenship; it handed him over to the police for overstaying his tourist visa by about six years. Viktor called me from prison to tell me he was about to be deported.

There was nothing I, or anyone else, could do. They put Viktor, dressed in his black suit and hat with prayer fringes dangling down, on a plane and sent him back where he came from.

This story has a happy ending. In Bucharest, Viktor was befriended by an influential Romanian rabbi with a bad back. Viktor gave him massage therapy and received a letter of recommendation in return. This rabbi was from the right party, and the letter did the trick. Eventually Viktor was allowed to return to Israel and, after undergoing a second, "official" conversion by a politically connected rabbinical court, he was permitted to stay. It took him almost eight years, but he was kosher.

In the United States, where religion is a personal matter not regulated by the government, conversions are much easier. In Miami, twenty years ago, I knew a rabbi named Emmet Frank who offered a one-day conversion course complete with ritual immersion on the beach. But even Rabbi Frank made his candidates spend eight hours in the classroom (time off for lunch). He also provided them with a warranty. "If you forget something, call me at home," he told the newly minted Jews.

Most of Rabbi Frank's customers—like many mainstream Reform and Conservative converts—have very little interest in Judaism as a religion. They are appeasers of Jewish in-laws (or, in some cases, rebels against their own Christian families). Orthodox converts are expected to take on "the burden of the Torah." Conservatives are required to serve kosher food at the conversion party. Reform converts are encouraged not to practice other religions. But no one gets into the tribe, let alone heaven, with a cell phone call to the secretary.

CHRISTIAN ZIONISTS TEND to downplay the degree to which converting Jews is important to them. This is especially true when they are dealing with the Israeli government, which, because of the pivotal importance of its clerical political parties, is sensitive to the Orthodox horror of missionaries. This, in turn, sometimes leads to misunderstandings. That's what happened to Pastor John Hagee in early 2006 in San Antonio, Texas.

No Christian Zionist in the United States is more red hot than Hagee. The Pentecostal pastor of the Cornerstone Church has traveled to Israel often, supported a succession of Israeli prime ministers, raised millions of dollars for Russian Jewish immigrants, and written best-selling books of Israel advocacy. Zionism is at the very heart of his ministry. Hagee's website boasts of an honorary doctorate from an institution called the Netanya Academic College and brags that he is the first gentile ever to receive the San Antonio B'nai B'rith Humanitarian of the Year Award.

On February 7, 2006—which Hagee calls "a historic day in the history of Christianity in America"—he made a bid to put himself into the front rank of Christian Zionism by inviting three hundred clergymen and lay leaders from around the country to gather in San Antonio for the purpose of founding Christians United for Israel. CUFI's declared purpose is to be "a national organization through which every pro-Israel organization and ministry in America can speak and act in one voice in support of Israel in matters related to Biblical issues."

Among the clergymen in attendance that day was Aryeh Scheinberg, an Orthodox rabbi in San Antonio and a longtime friend and collaborator of Hagee's. Attempting to explain what the group was all about to a reporter from the *Jerusalem Post,* Scheinberg said that Hagee does not believe in proselytizing Jews because Jews have a separate covenant with God. Scheinberg also told the reporter that it was safe to infer that Jerry Falwell felt the same way.

Neither the rabbi nor the Israeli reporter understood the implications of this claim. If Scheinberg was right, two of the nation's leading fundamentalist preachers were accepting the doctrine of "dual covenant"—common among some liberal Protestant denominations, but heretical to evangelicals—which holds that Jews can go to heaven without Christian salvation.

The *Post* story set off a firestorm in the evangelical world.

Falwell immediately issued a denial. "I have been on record all 54 years of my ministry as being opposed to 'dual covenant' theology," he wrote. "I simply can't alter my deeply held belief in the exclusivity of salvation through the Gospel of Christ for the sake of political or theological expediency. Like the Apostle Paul I pray daily for the salvation of everyone, including the Jewish people."

Hagee, for his part, sent a letter to the editor of the *Jerusalem Post* affirming that if Jews inquire about Christianity, "we give them a full scriptural presentation of redemption as presented in scripture. Regardless of the response from the Jewish person, we remain friends in support of the State of Israel as required by scripture."

Rabbi Scheinberg had inadvertently let an evangelical cat out of the bag. Falwell, Hagee, and other advocates of Judeo-Christian partnership had, over the years, adopted what amounts to a "don't ask, don't tell" policy in dealing with Jews. For evangelical Zionists, it is the price of admission with Israeli politicians, and it is based on the tacit assumption that, in the matter of the conversion of the Jews, God will work things out for himself.

PASTOR ANN STRATTON doesn't practice "don't ask, don't tell." She tells. An Italian Catholic girl from New Jersey turned Manhattan Pentecostal faith healer, she looks and sounds like Adrianna in *The Sopranos*, and her approach to salvation is along the lines of an offer you can't refuse.

I met Pastor Ann and her husband, Pastor Dan Stratton, on a brilliant September Sunday morning in 2005 just a week after they had moved into the new premises of the Faith Exchange Church of Tribeca. The "Exchange" refers to Wall Street, where Dan—Yale, Skull and Bones, all-Ivy tight-end class of '81—once scored a $453,000 commission as a commodities broker in a single day, took it as a sign from God, and began to preach the Bible to his fellow traders.

Around that time Dan met Ann in a nightclub. She was there, she says, looking for a soul to save and a man to marry. "I used to pray to God to give me a husband. Let's just say that before I met Dan, God sent me a lot of guys to minister to."

Dan and Ann got married, received Pentecostal ordination

from Oral Roberts, and started a church on Wall Street that was obliterated on 9/11. For a long time their congregation met in the Marriott Hotel in the Financial Center. Now they had found what they hoped would be a permanent downtown home, the former headquarters of the Tribeca Film Festival no less, and they were in a celebratory mood.

One of the best things about a Pentecostal church in Manhattan is the quality of the music. The Faith Exchange band featured Billy "Spaceman" Patterson, a New York guitar legend who has played with Miles Davis and James Brown. The choir was mostly off-Broadway talent. The chow is another bonus: after services the Strattons took me to the Tribeca Café for brunch.

Pastor Dan was mostly interested in talking real estate.

He had been through a harrowing few years trying to find a New York landlord willing to rent a ground-floor property to a Pentecostal church in the general environs of Wall Street. He attributed this resistance to Satan. Pastor Ann, whose specialties include biblical nutrition (no shrimp!), let Dan do most of the talking. It is an article of faith among evangelicals that, as the Bible says, "God put man at the head."

But Ann has strongly felt opinions, especially on the subject of conversion. At the start of his ministry, Dan had tried to reach out to the Jewish brokers he worked with. "Their books were not my books," he said philosophically. This lack of response has given him a decidedly laissez-faire approach. "If the truth convinces you, so be it," he said, swallowing a tight-end-sized portion of Spanish omelet.

Pastor Ann didn't want to leave it there. "You have no idea how much we love Jews in New Jersey," she said.

I thought about all the great Garden State yid-wop collaborations: Abner "Longy" Zwillman (aka "the Al Capone of Newark") and his associate Willie Moretti; Harold "Kayo" Konigsberg and his boss, Anthony "Tony Pro" Provenzano of the Teamsters. Even the Hebrew University in Jerusalem has a Sinatra Building.

"There's love there, no doubt," I said. "But love doesn't get you into heaven."

"Look, that's not the case," said Pastor Ann. "God loves Jews so much that he has a special deal for them. Here's how it goes. The *instant* before a Jew is about to die, Jesus appears right before his eyes and gives him one last chance to repent and accept salvation."

"And what if he doesn't want to repent and become a Christian?" It was the same question I had asked Sue Ricksecker, the secretary at Emmanuel Baptist, a few months earlier. But Pastor Ann had a Jersey answer. She fixed me a direct stare and said, "If Jesus shows up on your *death*bed? Come on. What are ya gonna do—tell him to get lost?"

FIVE

DOC AND THE PAT

There are hundreds of conservative Christian institutions of higher learning all over the United States, but the cradle of evangelical education is Virginia, home to both Liberty University in Lynchburg and Regent University in Virginia Beach. These schools owe their importance to their respective founders, Jerry Falwell, known to his students as Doc, and "The Pat," Pat Robertson. They are the Ruth and Gehrig of Zionist evangelism, the first truly big hitters. In the fall of 2005, I went south to see the universities they have built.

THE MUNICIPAL SLOGAN of Lynchburg is engraved on the tile floor of its modest airport: "The most interesting spot in the state." This was the assessment of an early resident of the place, Thomas Jefferson, who also predicted that someday Lynchburg would be a great metropolis.

Jefferson, right about so much, was wrong about this. Lynchburg is a sleepy little town of 65,000 on the banks of the polluted James River. Its municipal website lists just two "Famous Products": the Fleet enema and the disposable douche. The website is discreetly silent about the fact that a local firm, Babcock & Wilcox, designed the nuclear reactor at Three Mile Island. And, oddly, there is no mention of Lynchburg's only national claim to fame: Liberty University.

The first thing you see when you enter the Liberty University visitors center is a museum dedicated to the life and times of Jerry Falwell, the institution's founder and chancellor. And the first thing you see in the museum is a Model T Ford. A mannequin dressed in 1920s gangster garb is loading illegal booze into the car. That man is supposed to be Reverend Falwell's father. Carey Falwell was a successful businessman who founded bus companies. He was also a hoodlum who, in addition to moonshining, organized illegal cock and dog fights and ran a notorious nightspot. In 1931, he shot and killed his own brother, Garland. The killing was ruled self-defense, but it cemented Carey Falwell's reputation in Lynchburg as a very bad man.

This sort of laundry is not usually hung in the personal museums of university founders, but Jerry Falwell is a born-again Christian and the exhibit is a witness to his belief that nobody—and nobody's son—is beyond salvation. It is also a slightly boastful reminder that Falwell may be a preacher, but he comes from tough entrepreneurial stock.

On a crisp fall day, bemused visitors wandered through the museum. They had come to campus with their kids to attend College-for-a-Weekend, a chance for prospective students to get a firsthand look at the university, founded by Falwell in 1971, on top of what is now called Liberty Mountain.

I had arrived in Lynchburg the night before and had breakfasted with some of these prospective students and other wayfarers at the Lynchburg Sleep Inn. Some of the customers looked like a rogues gallery of the Jewish imagination: Vietnam vets on the way home from a convention in Branson, Missouri; a couple of tattooed bikers; an old guy in a cowboy hat; and a woman in late middle age dressed like Aunt Bee on *The Andy Griffith Show.*

The Vietnam vets struck up a nostalgic army conversation with the guy in the cowboy hat, who had served in Korea. When they caught me listening in, I figured it was a good chance to sample local public opinion. "I was in the Israeli army," I said.

Heads turned. One of the bikers said, "I been there. In Ashdod. I was flying helicopters for the army and we had some dealings there. Y'all are some damn fine soldiers."

I smiled modestly.

Aunt Bee said, "What I admire most about you is how your girls serve in the army, right along with the boys."

"My daughter was in the army," I said. "My son, too."

"That's great," said the guy in the cowboy hat. "I live in San Antonio. You come down that way, I can introduce you to a lot of Jewish friends of mine."

When I got up to leave, one of the vets extended his hand. "It's been an honor to meet you," he said.

"The guys over there are damn good guys," said the helicopter pilot. I left the dining room in a hail of God-blesses and headed over to Liberty University.

JERRY FALWELL IS every bit the entrepreneur his father was. The school he started as a little Baptist college has grown into a sprawling 4,400-acre campus with around ten thousand students on the premises and thousands more enrolled in long-distance learning programs. Liberty offers fifteen graduate programs, and in 2004 it opened its own law school, which won an accreditation less than two years later. But it is proudest of its undergraduate program.

Liberty consistently scores among the top ten conservative

schools in the nation in the Young America's Foundation rankings, and if its aggregate college board scores don't threaten Harvard or Stanford, the school projects a definite sense of self-confidence and self-improvement. It now gets about twenty thousand applicants a year for its 3,200 freshman slots. Falwell expects to at least double its capacity in the next fifteen years. If he doesn't live to see it, his two sons will. Nepotism is common in the evangelical world. Pat Robertson, Oral Roberts, and Billy Graham have all positioned their sons to take over the leadership of their ministries. So has Falwell.

THERE WAS A time when Jerry Falwell raised most of his money in the mail, in response to his *Old Time Gospel Bible Hour* telecasts from the pulpit of the Thomas Road Baptist Church. According to his associates, there were days when the ministry took in $1 million in donations. But that kind of money dried up in the 1980s when one famous televangelist, Jimmy Swaggart, got caught with a hooker and another, Jim Bakker, not only disgraced himself in a sex scandal but defrauded his followers and went to jail. Falwell himself wasn't implicated—in fact, he played a role in trying to rescue Bakker's *Praise the Lord* enterprise—but many people stopped sending in checks to televangelists. "The money just dried up like somebody turned off the faucet," one of Falwell's assistants told me. This dire development may have contributed to Falwell's judgment that Bakker was "the greatest scab and cancer on the face of Christianity in two thousand years." It certainly changed his fund-raising strategy. His ministry began to rely on large gifts, some worth tens of millions of dollars. Liberty Mountain reflects that prosperity. Falwell's church is large enough to have its own mall, called Main Street. He runs a K–12 school whose graduates can attend Liberty University for free. The Liberty campus itself is dotted with construction sites, including the LaHaye Ice Rink, a professional-size hockey arena donated by the author of the Left Behind novels. Considering LaHaye's apocalyptic beliefs—and Falwell's own End of Days eschatology—I found this focus on the future reassuring.

ABOUT A THOUSAND prospective students (and almost twice as many parents) were on campus for College-for-a-Weekend. They looked like standard American teenagers, but the mere fact that they were considering Liberty University put them in a special category. The university is governed by a code of conduct called the Liberty Way, and it is not for kids looking for a party. Alcohol, tobacco, and drugs are strictly outlawed, and students are required to submit to random testing. Dancing, or even attending a dance, is forbidden. Movies rated R, NC-17, or X are unacceptable (the Liberty Way makes it clear this is not an automatic endorsement of movies rated PG or PG-13). Having an abortion can be grounds for expulsion. The same goes for "involvement with witchcraft, séances, or other occultic activities."

Liberty students under the age of twenty-one are required to live in gender-segregated dormitories where they are supervised by "prayer leaders." The dorms don't have cable or satellite television, and computers are filtered for pornography. During the week, curfew is midnight.

Political demonstrations of any sort are banned on campus unless they get explicit permission from the administration. Unauthorized written material may not be distributed.

Still, some old grads think that Liberty is going soft. A generation ago, male and female students weren't allowed to converse after six in the evening. Students couldn't leave campus without permission. The dress code was strict: ties for the men, modest dresses for the women (only this year have students been allowed to wear jeans to class). "Boys and girls can use the swimming pool together, provided the girls wear one-piece bathing suits," a Liberty alum in his forties told me. "Back in my time that wasn't permitted. Of course, back then we didn't have a swimming pool, either."

The Liberty Way is enforced not only by the faculty and the dorm leaders, but by the students themselves, in an honor system modeled on the military academies. Every class begins with a prayer. Students attend three mandatory chapel services each week.

Liberty is racially mixed, but not exactly what you'd call diverse. Faculty members are required to be professing Christians. "I'm sure there are some kids here who aren't saved," spokesman Don Egle told me. "And there must be some Democrats around, too. During the election I saw a few cars with Kerry stickers."

FALWELL HIMSELF HAS been a force in the Republican Party since he founded the Moral Majority in 1979. From the start he envisioned it as a political movement, not an ecclesiastical one, and he very much wanted to include Jews. "Critics of my ministry have tried to drive a wedge between me and the Jewish community around the country," he wrote in his autobiography. "They forgot that my master was a Jewish rabbi." The rabbi, obviously, was Jesus.

In 1957, when unknown enemies attacked Falwell's Thomas Road church, Jews came to his aid. The Schewel brothers of Lynchburg, who owned a large furniture business, wrote a check to repair and renovate the church. "They knew from their own Jewish heritage the problem of vandalism and wanted to express immediate and practical sympathy," writes Falwell. Years later, State Senator Elliot Schewel helped get Liberty University tax-exempt status.

Falwell—a major force in Lynchburg—has reciprocated by helping to make it a very pleasant place for Jews to live. "The philo-Semitism is sometimes over the top," says Rabbi Tom Gutherz, who was the chief (and only) rabbi of Lynchburg for twelve years. "Did I ever witness or experience any Christian anti-Semitism in Lynchburg? I can give an unconditional answer: No. Of course there's some garden variety anti-Semitism, like there is everywhere, but specifically Christian? None. Zero. And the Lynchburg city council and school board have been good about respecting the separation between church and state." I heard similar sentiments from rabbis and Jews from towns all over the Bible Belt.

Gutherz never had a problem with missionaries, either.

"The whole time I was in Lynchburg, we didn't have a single Jew who converted to Christianity. The opposite is true; we had Christians who converted to Judaism."

Rabbi Gutherz is a liberal, and no fan of Jerry Falwell's politics. But he encountered nothing but religious respect from Liberty University. "Falwell encourages his students to be positive about us," said Gutherz. "They even came sometimes to our Friday-night services. In some way they saw us as fellow people of God. They didn't understand the prayers in Hebrew, but they saw us as part of their tradition, something like 'that old time religion.'"

FALWELL ESTABLISHED THE Moral Majority on four principles: "Pro-life, pro-traditional family, pro-moral and pro-American (including a strong national defense), and support for the State of Israel." This set the stage for Israeli prime minister Menachem Begin to join the Schewel family of Lynchburg in Falwell's pantheon of Jewish amigos.

Begin had no problem with Falwell's first three principles—he was all for life (although abortion was never a political issue for him), family (his own campaign ads in 1977 called him a "family man"), and a strong American military posture in the cold war (his experience in a Soviet gulag during World War II had made him strongly anticommunist). And he positively loved point number four.

It is a myth that Begin gave Falwell a private jet. The prime minister of Israel doesn't have planes to give away. Begin himself flew El Al and he would have gone coach if his security detail had let him. What he gave Falwell was access and friendship.

Falwell reciprocated. In 1981, he invited Begin to speak at Liberty, and he planned a royal reception, complete with the student body lined up along the route to campus, singing the Israeli national anthem. Begin's wife got sick and the visit was canceled, but Falwell still smiles at the thought of what might have been, a mass of born-again undergraduates filling the Blue Ridge Mountains with the sounds of "HaTikvah."

Falwell has maintained ties with every Israeli prime minister since Begin. He tried to aid Yitzhak Shamir in the face of George H. W. Bush's coolness toward the Jewish state, and helped Prime Minister Benjamin Netanyahu withstand Bill Clinton's pressure on the extent of Israeli withdrawals from the West Bank.

"We were in Manila," recalls Duke Westover, Falwell's longtime major domo. "We got a call from Jerusalem, from Bibi Netanyahu. President Clinton had summoned him to Washington to discuss concessions, and Bibi didn't want to go, but it was a command performance. He asked if we could put together a meeting with evangelical supporters of Israel before he went to the White House."

Falwell gave the order and Westover began calling pastors and activists in the United States. "We had three, four days to put it together," he recalls. "Somehow, we made it. When Bibi got to Washington, we had fifteen hundred evangelicals waiting for him in the ballroom of the Mayflower Hotel. Not just folks, either, pastors and leaders. It was the first time that an Israeli prime minister ever came to the United States and met with Christian supporters before he met with Jewish leaders."

What happened next is a story Falwell likes to tell. "Next day, Bibi went into the Oval Office and Clinton said, 'I know who you were with last night.' But before the meeting went much further, an aide came in, gave Clinton a message, and Clinton turned white. That was the day the Monica Lewinsky scandal broke."

Falwell liked Bibi, and he liked Ariel Sharon. "Sharon was a good man," he told me. "I personally had a problem with trading land for peace but that's not our business. If Sharon wanted to say no to a withdrawal, okay, we would have supported him. And if he said yes, well, that's okay with me, too. Israel operates on very thin margins of error. I trust Israeli leaders to know what they're doing."

In 1999, Falwell found another way to express his Zionism. He sent his entire freshman class—fifteen hundred students—to Israel on a ten-day tour. "I want our students to love Israel and to understand why supporting it is sacred," he told me.

Thanks largely to Falwell and Pat Robertson, this level of evangelical Zionist enthusiasm now seems self-evident. But it is not. "We didn't talk much about the Jews, or Israel, in the 1950s," Falwell recalled. "It wasn't an issue. My kids' generation has a positive attitude toward Israel and Jews, far more than mine did. And that's not going to change. Places like Liberty University will see to it."

THE CENTERPIECE OF College-for-a-Weekend was a giant convocation in the Vines Center, the university's eleven-thousand-seat cathedral cum basketball arena. I sat in the back, a missionary family from Turkey on one side, an Italian-Catholic from Bensonhurst turned born-again Baptist on the other. Over the stage, a banner proclaiming "God's Way to Heaven: John 16:4" hung next to a giant KFC sign bearing a likeness of the Colonel. A Christian rock band warmed up the crowd. Once upon a time Baptist preachers like Jerry Falwell denounced rock and roll as Satan's music, but contemporary evangelical Christianity is nothing if not showbiz savvy.

Falwell took the podium with the electric guitar still reverberating in the auditorium. He opened with reflections on the meaning of November 22, 1963. "Three men died that day," he said. "John F. Kennedy, Aldous Huxley, and C. S. Lewis." Huxley, the atheist author of *Brave New World*, went out, according to Falwell, full of dread and drugs; C. S. Lewis, the Christian novelist and thinker, died peacefully, convinced he was on his way to heaven. Most of the kids barely knew who JFK was, let alone Aldous Huxley. C. S. Lewis they had heard of; one of his Narnia books, *The Lion, the Witch, and the Wardrobe,* had been made into a movie and was getting a lot of Hollywood hype.

Falwell preached about Christian values in the midst of a holy war. "Todd Beamer was a hero," he said. "He fought the terrorists on Flight 93 and maybe saved the White House or the Capitol. And I don't call these terrorists 'insurgents' either. They are barbarians!"

The crowd cheered.

"Todd Beamer was a committed Christian," said Falwell. "And when he knew he was going to die, he made one phone call. He called home."

Falwell told the students that God was both their best friend and the creator of the universe. "You have to be unintelligent not to believe in intelligent design. I believe in the Second Coming," he said. "I am a premillennialist Baptist. In the last part of the Bible, we *win*. I've lived through Naziism, communism, and, now, Islamic terrorism. In Jordan the other day, the barbarians bombed a wedding in a hotel because, they said, they thought there would be Americans and Jews there. Isn't it terrible to be filled with such hate? But there is no panic button here. God is in control! We win!"

WINNING IS IMPORTANT to Falwell. He is a naturally competitive man, and he revels in victory. The Liberty debate team is his pride and joy.

"Our football program can't change the culture," he told me. "Our debate program can, by producing advocates who know how to argue for Judeo-Christian ethics and the American Constitution. We have thirty-two kids on our team this year and they'll all be lawyers or leaders of some sort. Our goal is to create advocates who know how to make their case. These are brilliant, articulate students. I couldn't have made the Liberty debate team when I was that age. I couldn't talk that fast."

"We're Doc's baby," said debate coach Brett O'Donnell, referring to Falwell by his Liberty nickname. "He follows our schedule. The kids know we matter to him."

Liberty's program has five full-time coaches and a budget of half a million dollars—a small fortune in the world of collegiate debate. Falwell doesn't want just winners, he wants champions for Christ. O'Donnell produces: Liberty is a perennial debate power. In 2006, it came in first in all three national rankings.

Every year, O'Donnell sends out a flyer to all incoming freshmen with college boards over 1200—about 15 percent of the class. A few dozen reply, and he puts them through a boot camp during the first week of school. Eight or ten novices make it through, and they are treated as an elite.

"We don't compete against Mount Pisgah College, we debate Harvard," Falwell told me proudly.

A few years ago, the national debate topic dealt with abortion. Under the rules, teams were required to argue both sides, and this presented a problem. Some evangelical colleges dropped debate. Not Liberty.

"Doc decided that if we wanted to compete, we'd need to accept the rules," O'Donnell says. That season, by special dispensation, Liberty's debate practice rooms became the only place on campus where students were free to argue in favor of *Roe v. Wade.*

According to O'Donnell, one of Liberty's great advantages is that, despite its success, it is consistently underestimated. "We're supposed to be dumb," he said. "People take us lightly. And I won't lie, that gets the kids motivated. We get a lot of pleasure when we beat a Columbia or a Dartmouth. But the point is not to develop one or two superstars. We want to educate a lot of kids, an army of kids, and instill them with a sense of mission."

IF LIBERTY UNIVERSITY is a hotbed of evangelical populism, its neighbor to the south, Pat Robertson's Regent University, is the home of elite Pentecostalism. Located in Virginia Beach, four hours east of Lynchburg, Regent is half the size of Liberty University and twice as grand. Falwell's school seems to be growing wild out of the mountains and overflows with energy. The Regent campus is as mannered and manicured as a country club. The architecture is Georgian, hand-hewn brick and arched windows; the interiors glisten with polished mahogany and marble.

Visitors to Regent don't stay at the local Sleep-Inn, either. The university's Founders Inn is a high-end spa and resort. Its boutique sells Italian fashions, not evangelical souvenirs. And, despite the protests of some of Robertson's supporters, fine wines are available in the Hunt Room.

In his autobiography, Falwell contrasts his own humble origins with "my friend Pat Robertson [who] traces his roots in Virginia from the chaplain of the first permanent English-speaking settlement in the new world, through a signer of the Declaration of Independence, an officer on George Washington's staff, two American presidents, and his own father, our distinguished, long-term Senator from Virginia."

Falwell was being polite. Robertson's father, A. Willis Robertson, served in the House of Representatives from 1933 to 1946, and then in the Senate until 1966, and it is hard to point to a single word or deed of his that could be fairly called distinguished. The old man was a standard-issue Southern Democratic segregationist: no worse than the others and no better. This hasn't stopped "The Pat," as the students call him, from honoring his father by naming the Regent School of Government after him.

YOU DON'T JUST drop in on Regent University. There is a guard at the gate who directs you to the administration building, and if you have business on the campus you get a guide. Mine was a friendly woman named Diane, who led me to meetings with members of the faculty. When I snuck off to browse through the student bookstore, a call from the suspicious saleswoman brought Diane running.

But the salient aspects of Regent University are evident to even the supervised eye. The campus is dominated by powerful television transmitters and Robertson's magisterial home, complete with stables and horses. Regent is a Virginia plantation that grows and exports Pentecostalism, and business is good. Robertson recently opened a second campus near Washington, D.C., and he has far-flung charities. Still, the Big House at the center of the Virginia Beach campus is the heart of the enterprise. When I visited, Robertson was holed up there ("He's busy writing a *book,*" an awestruck administrator said), although he could be spotted riding in the mornings.

Robertson was born a fortunate son, but he made his own money. After a stint in the Marine Corps, where he was, by all accounts, a hail-fellow-well-met, he graduated from Yale Law School, flunked the bar exam, got converted by a Dutch preacher named Cornelius Vanderbreggen, was ordained as a Baptist minister, and, in 1960, bought a little UHF station in Portsmouth, Virginia. Robertson parlayed this into the Christian Broadcasting Network and became America's first great evangelical television mogul. In 1997 he sold International Family Entertainment, including the Family Channel, to Fox Kids Worldwide for $1.9 billion. He kept the 700 Club, which continues to pull in roughly a million viewers a day.

As a TV host, Robertson can be genial and engaging, but erratic. The day of my visit, the voters of Dover, Pennsylvania, had turned out schoolboard members who favored teaching intelligent design. This infuriated Robertson. "I'd like to say to the good citizens of Dover, if there is a disaster in your area, don't turn to God. You just rejected him from your city," he said on TV. "Pat does pop off," Regent professor Joe Kickasola said ruefully. "But that's just Pat being Pat."

ROBERTSON HAS A long history of making bizarre claims, like controlling the weather and healing tonsillitis over the tube. He's famous for saying nasty things about homosexuals, the prophet Muhammad, Hindus, mainline Protestants, liberals, feminists, political rivals, and foreign leaders who have offended him. In the summer of 2005, he called for the assassination of the anti-American president of Venezuela, Hugo Chavez. Robertson's critics have always thought he was out of his mind, but now a lot of evangelicals think so too.

The faculty of Regent is discreet, as befits men and women who live on the goodwill of the Big House, but the students, most of whom have never met him, seem almost proud of his eccentricities, like kids with the craziest uncle on the block.

JEWS ARE ONE of the few groups that Robertson approves of. In his 1988 presidential run, he promised that all his appointees would be either Christians (by which, presumably, he meant religious Christians) or Jews (degree of religiosity unspecified). When he was challenged on this, he simply said that America is a Judeo-Christian country and people who didn't like that would have to learn to live with it. He might have added that *no* president has ever appointed a Hindu, a Muslim, or a Buddhist to a cabinet position, but he wasn't making the point that there is a lot of hypocrisy in the theory and practice of political diversity; he was simply defending his belief that the United States is a Christian nation, and that Christianity flows from Judaism.

ROBERTSON WAS ONE of the first evangelists to offer the Judeo-Christian bargain to American Jews. And, like Falwell, he also reached out to Israel. "Looking back thirty years, I'm convinced that evangelical support for Israel wouldn't have been so broad without Pat Robertson," says Rabbi Yechiel Eckstein of the International Fellowship of Christians and Jews. "He and Jerry Falwell were the first to really stand up. When the time came to sign ads against the American sale of advanced warplanes to Saudi Arabia during the Reagan administration, Billy Graham wouldn't sign but Robertson and Falwell did. Because of them, Christian support for Israel went from a tendency to a movement."

But movements can get out of hand. In January 2006, Robertson demonstrated that there's such a thing as being too pro-Israel, even for Israelis.

Following Prime Minister Ariel Sharon's incapacitating stroke, Robertson told the audience of the 700 Club that the Israeli premier had been struck down for giving up biblical Jewish settlements in the Gaza Strip and northern Samaria. "He was dividing God's land. And I would say, 'Woe unto any prime minister of Israel who takes a similar course to appease the EU, the United Nations, or the United States of America. God says, 'This land belongs to me. You better leave it alone.'"

The Israeli government reacted with ostensible fury. In fact, nobody was too shocked by Robertson's comments; right-wing Israeli rabbis had been saying similar things for years. Not long before, a small band of Israeli fanatics had even put a *pulsa d'nura*—an ancient kabbalistic curse—on Sharon's life (this is the same curse that was cast on Prime Minister Yitzhak Rabin before he was assassinated by a fanatic yeshiva student in 1995).

Still, Israeli politicians from Sharon's recently formed Kadima Party felt the need to respond to Robertson. The prime minister had gone into a coma politically intestate. His potential heirs needed to defend his good name.

The minister of tourism, Avraham Hirschson, had, for months, been trying to involve Robertson and other evangelical businessmen in a project to develop a tourist center on the northern banks of the Sea of Galilee, near the Mount of Beatitudes and Capernaum. The Americans were supposedly putting together a $50 million investment, a tidy sum by Israeli standards, but Hirschson, a close ally of prime minister-to-be Ehud Olmert, publicly pulled the plug. "We will not do business with [Robertson]," he said, through his spokesman. "We will deal only with other evangelicals who don't back these comments."

In reality, there were no other investors. The whole deal was still in the talking stage. But the slap from Jerusalem stung Robertson, who sent a letter of apology to Sharon's sons. "I ask your forgiveness and the forgiveness of the people of Israel for remarks I made at the time concerning the writing of the holy prophet Joel and his view of the inviolate nature of the land of Israel," he wrote. "I pray for the future of your country, and when I speak it is always as a friend."

The apology was accepted. By this time it had become clear that Sharon wasn't going to wake up and be offended by Robertson's comments (he wouldn't have been anyway; Sharon was an amused connoisseur of crazy Israeli political clerics). Hirschson let it be known that he might even be willing to reconsider letting Robertson invest.

THE SIMPLE FACT is that, nuts or not, Robertson is a man with his own university, an army of lawyers, and a million viewers a day. In short, he's a good man to have on your side. At a conference in Israel, in 2003, he spelled out the rationale for the evangelical love of Israel he has spent a career fostering.

> Of course, we, like all right-thinking people, support Israel because Israel is an island of democracy, an island of individual freedom, an island of the rule of law, and an island of modernity in the midst of a sea of dictatorial regimes, the suppression of individual liberty, and a fanatical religion intent on returning to the feudalism of 8th Century Arabia. These facts about modern day Israel are all true. But mere political rhetoric does not account for the profound devotion to Israel that exists in the hearts of tens of millions of evangelical Christians.
>
> You must realize that the God who spoke to Moses on

Mount Sinai is our God. Abraham, Isaac, and Jacob are our spiritual Patriarchs. Jeremiah, Ezekiel, and Daniel are our prophets. King David, a man after God's own heart, is our hero. The Holy City of Jerusalem is our spiritual capital. And the continuation of Jewish sovereignty over the Holy Land is a further bulwark to us that the God of the Bible exists and that His Word is true. . . .

We are with you in your struggle. We are with you as a wave of anti-Semitism is engulfing the earth. We are with you despite the pressure of the "Quartette" and the incredibly hostile resolutions of the United Nations. We are with you despite the threats and ravings of Wahabbi Jihadists, Hezbollah thugs, and Hamas assassins.

We are with you despite oil embargos, loss of allies, and terrorist attacks on our cities.

We evangelical Christians merely say to our Israeli friends, "Let us serve our God together by opposing the virulent poison of anti-Semitism and anti-Zionism that is rapidly engulfing the world."

It is easy to dismiss Robertson as a crank. And it is true that he, Falwell, and the generation of Christian Zionists they have produced lack the style and nuance of liberal Christians and secular intellectuals. On the other hand, Robertson has had no trouble recognizing Islamic radicalism when he sees it, and no hesitation about confronting it. There is something to be said for ideology that produces this kind of clarity and courage. There is certainly something to be said for it by Jews at a time when the Jewish state is under attack not only by Islamic holy warriors but by liberal Christian fellow travelers as well.

SIX

REVENGE OF THE MAINLINE

It's hard to remember, but during World War II, Zionism was a popular left-wing Christian cause. In 1942, celebrity theologians Reinhold Niebuhr and Paul Tillich joined the liberal Christian Council on Palestine (meaning, in those days, *Jewish* Palestine) in arguing that the establishment of a Jewish state was both an urgent humanitarian need and an act of justice. In 1949 Niebuhr opposed a demand by the Vatican that Jerusalem be internationalized (Israel considered the city its capital). Reverend Adam Clayton Powell Jr., the firebrand liberal pastor of Harlem's mammoth Abyssinian Baptist Church, actually appeared at a Madison Square Garden fund-raising rally for Menachem Begin's Irgun faction.

But when Zionism went from theory to fact, it started to trouble liberal Christians. The newly formed World Council of Churches' first statement on the subject, in 1949, was a masterpiece of double-talk. "On the political aspects of the Palestine problem and the complex conflict of 'rights' involved we do not undertake to express a judgment. Nevertheless, we appeal to the nations to deal with the problem not as one of expediency—political, strategic or economic—but as a moral and spiritual question that touches a nerve centre of the world's religious life."

It was downhill from there, and things hit bottom after the Six-Day War of 1967. Liberation theology, just coming into vogue, saw Western societies as colonialist oppressors, and the Jews of Israel received a post–World War II racial upgrade for the purpose of guilt-sharing. Many liberal Christians—in Europe even more than the United States—were pleased to conclude that, given half a chance, Jews would behave just as badly as everyone else (and worse, really, because the Jews should know better).

This hostility to Israel struck American Jews—who saw the Six-Day War as a great victory and a huge relief—as a hard blow. Liberal Protestants were their social role models and political allies. They had marched together in Selma and against the war in Vietnam. As David Elcott of the American Jewish Committee put it, mainline Christians were "rational Americans, whom we respect in so many ways, who were educated in the same schools as we, knew the facts we presented [about the Arab-Israel conflict] and saw the whole scene differently."

As evangelical support for Israel grew, and the Catholic-Israeli relationship improved during the papacy of John Paul II, who visited the Holy Land and called Jews "our elder brothers," activists in the mainline churches became constant critics of Israel. Jewish lobbyists like Elcott, who worked with Christian liberals for years on every item of the domestic agenda, found themselves suffering through long, strained silences when the subject turned to the Jewish state.

Several factors explain this split. One, perhaps the most important, is theological, centered around the nature of the Second Coming.

All conventional Protestant denominations recognize Jesus as the Messiah and believe he will return. They differ, however, over two critical questions: When is he coming, and why?

Liberals tend to believe that Jesus will return as a result of

mankind's efforts. When people are sufficiently virtuous, a messianic age will be ushered in. In this view, known as postmillennial-
ism, every house built for Habitat for Humanity, every hot meal
served at a downtown soup kitchen, every human rights document signed at the United Nations, helps speed up the arrival of
the Messiah. Good deeds are not simply a moral imperative, they
are an instrument of meta-history.

Evangelicals see things differently. It says in the Bible that the
Messiah is returning, and while even the most pious evangelicals
tend to be agnostic about when, they have no doubt he's on his
way. "I believe Jesus is coming to clean up all the messes," says
Jerry Falwell. In the evangelical, premillennialist worldview, Jesus
is the *agent* of perfection, not its beneficiary. He will come in his
own good time, a schedule that can't be hurried along by human
efforts.

For many years this belief caused evangelicals to turn inward.
What was the point of trying to change things, after all, if Jesus
was going to do it anyway? What mattered was individual salvation, getting right with God. When the burst of evangelical political activism represented by 1920s Prohibition failed, conservative
Protestants retreated to their churches, where they were taught
that religion and politics don't mix.

Jerry Falwell and Pat Robertson changed that. They believed
that whatever God had planned for the End of Days, people had a
right to live in the here and now according to their own values.
Politically they began as Democratic segregationists, but by the
time they reached political maturity they had become integration-
ists (evangelical churches today tend to be far more racially mixed
than upper-class Protestant denominations) and Republican.
Their conservatism was expressed mostly on family issues, especially opposition to abortion and what they regarded as libertine
sexual practices.

As evangelicals moved to the right, the mainline churches, once known as "the Republican Party at prayer," grew more politically liberal. By the start of the 1970s liberal Christian activists were an integral part of the Democratic coalition. This partisan reversal was accompanied by a demographic shift. Since the 1930s, mainline churches had dominated Protestant life. When Billy Graham brought his crusade to New York in the mid-1950s, he was ostentatiously snubbed by Reinhold Niebuhr. But such snobbery was only effective so long as the evangelicals were a quiescent minority. When they began voting as a bloc, it became apparent that they were more of a political force than the mainliners. By the mid-1970s, when the Gallup Poll first asked, "Would you describe yourself as born-again and/or an Evangelical Christian?" about 40 percent of Americans answered affirmatively. Now it was the mainline denominations that were on the defensive, and they didn't like it.

AMONG THE MANY issues that separated the evangelicals and the mainliners was their attitude toward Israel (and, by extension, Israel's Jewish supporters in the United States).

A few born-again figures, such as Jimmy Carter, Florida televangelist D. James Kennedy, and "progressive" Jim Wallis, took the Palestinian side of the dispute, but were, and remain, a distinct minority among the pro-Israel evangelicals. The social action wing of the mainline churches, on the other hand, grew ever more hostile to Israel through the 1980s and 1990s.

Just how hostile became apparent in the fall of 2000, when the second Palestinian intifada erupted. That summer, at Camp David, President Clinton and Prime Minister Ehud Barak offered the Palestinians a deal they thought Yasir Arafat couldn't refuse—an independent state in most of the West Bank and Gaza. Arafat surprised them by turning it down and starting a war, the second intifada. Arafat represented not just the Arabs of the West Bank and Gaza but the entire Palestinian people, a large number of whom did not live in the occupied territories. They were in Lebanon, Jordan, Syria, and beyond: refugees (and their descendants) of the 1948 War of Independence, displaced from pre-1967 Israel. Their demand was for a "right of return" to their old homes, not in the West Bank and Gaza but in Israel proper. This would have potentially created an Arab majority in Israel or, put another way, the end of Israel as a Jewish state. Obviously, Israel couldn't say yes, and didn't. But many of the mainline activists supported this Palestinian demand.

During the intifada, American Jews, even many on the left, rallied to Israel's side. So did the broader American public. The pro-Palestinian liberal Christian activist faction counterattacked with an ugly weapon: economic disinvestment.

In July 2004, the Presbyterian Church (USA) voted to "study" diverting the money in its church portfolio from some companies doing business with Israel. A few months later, the Episcopal Church voted for "year-long study" of the feasibility of boycotting companies linked to the "Israeli occupation." Shortly thereafter, the international policy body of the Anglican Church (to which the Episcopalians are affiliated) called on other denominations to undertake similar "studies."

In June 2005, the Virginia and New England conferences of the United Methodist Church approved resolutions calling for an investigation into whether they had holdings in companies that profited from Israel's occupation. A month later, the General Synod of the United Church of Christ voted to examine ways of using "economic leverage" to influence the Palestinian-Israeli dispute.

The campaign of divestment was not a real economic threat;

the Israeli economy is too large, and church investment too small. The power of divestment was symbolic. It had been a tool in the international campaign to discredit the apartheid regime in South Africa. It was a way of calling into question Israel's essential morality.

American Jews, especially liberals, were incensed. If Israel was South Africa, then what were they, its supporters? The Jewish establishment attempted to explain to their Protestant counterparts that Israel wasn't just another issue for them, but the very heart of their agenda. They expected their fellow liberals, who wanted and counted on Jewish support on *their* core social issues, would drop, or at least modify, support for Israel's enemies.

The mainstreamers turned this request down flat. They couldn't abandon the Palestinian cause, they explained, because it was "just." But like all moralistic political explanations, "justice" was code for a much more complex set of motives.

First, the Christian liberals believe that the meek shall inherit the earth—especially the earth where Jesus lived and taught. In their view, the Palestinians were the weaker party to the conflict, and this, automatically, located justice on their side.

"Israel power is a far more significant issue [to the liberal Protestants] than the pain caused by [Arab] terrorism," David Elcott wrote in an internal American Jewish Committee memorandum. "To make this point and correct the imbalance, Israel must be humbled and the suffering Palestinians exalted."

Second, liberal Protestants, no less than evangelicals, feel emotionally connected to the Holy Land. "When I see Bethlehem surrounded by Israeli troops, it moves me as a Christian," I was told by Canon Brian Grieves, the director of Peace and Ministries for the Episcopal Church and a leader of the pro-Palestinian forces.

Liberal denominations also have self-interested motives. The Anglican Church, for example, has a cathedral, Saint George's, in the eastern (Arab) part of Jerusalem. Presbyterians and other denominations own tracts of choice land in the Galilee. Everyone has real estate in Bethlehem. Christian Arabs are a small and shrinking minority among the Palestinians, but some of their ministers have forged strong links with the mainstream American denominations. Foremost among them is Reverend Naim Ateek, a Palestinian theologian who heads the Sabeel Ecumenical Liberation Theology Center in Jerusalem.

Mainline denominations also have constituencies—and missionary aspirations—in the wider Arab and Islamic world. A strong anti-Israel (or as they would prefer to have it seen, pro-Palestinian) bias is a way of ensuring goodwill in anti-Semitic countries where it is necessary to have government permission to function.

In other words, mainline Protestant activists have a rooting interest in the Arab-Israel conflict that goes beyond the pure pursuit of "justice." If American Jews instinctively support their coreligionists in Israel, these Christian liberals feel—and want to encourage—a similar sense of solidarity with *their* side.

The decline of the mainline church in America also plays a role.

According to pollster John Green, there are now nearly twice as many evangelicals as mainline Protestants, and "progressives" are a minority within the mainline minority. Not unnaturally, progressives have sought allies beyond the borders of the United States, especially within the framework of the international, mostly anti-American World Council of Churches.

At the WCC Assembly held in Porto Alegre, Brazil, in February 2006, the American delegation, representing thirty-four mainline Protestant and Orthodox denominations, issued an extraordinary "apology" to the world for the villainy of the United States. "Our leaders turned a deaf ear to the voices of church leaders throughout our nation and the world, entering into imperial projects that seek to dominate and control for the sake of our own national interests," the American delegation proclaimed. They accused the United States of "raining down terror" and begged forgiveness for the "violence, degradation and poverty our nation has sown. . . . Nations have been demonized and God has been enlisted in national agendas that are nothing short of idolatrous." For people who feel such a strong animus toward the United States, Israel's status as America's best friend in the Middle East is not a character reference.

Finally, and I hesitate to mention it, there is a possibility that some of the anti-Zionist clerics of the mainline churches harbor a tiny, un-Christian resentment toward Jews who have, to a large extent, replaced them in the country's cultural, intellectual, and political elite. "A couple of years ago the heads of the Methodist Church came to us and asked us to set up a meeting for them with President Bush," one Jewish lobbyist told me. "And Bush is a *Methodist*. I can't imagine they liked that very much."

IN SEPTEMBER 2005, a delegation of Jewish and Christian liberal activists undertook a "peace pilgrimage" to the Holy Land. Ostensibly they went looking for ways to foster harmony between the Palestinians and the Israelis. In fact, they were searching for a means of making peace among themselves or, as David Elcott put it, their competing "narratives."

"We [Jews] see ourselves as the ultimate victims, witness to the Holocaust," Elcott told me before the trip. "We feel that our suffering is being ignored by Christians who we assume are our friends."

Elcott's Christian friends, including Canon Grieves, had a narrative of their own, in which it is the Palestinians who are victims, the Israelis the victimizers. The question was, could these two versions of reality be reconciled?

The trip was carefully structured. Each side hosted an equal number of days. The Jews used their time to walk their liberal Christian counterparts through Old Testament history (Message: *We Jews were here first*), introduce them to Israeli victims of terror (*Arabs don't fight fair*), visit the Supreme Court in Jerusalem (*Israel is a democracy and a nation of laws*), travel along the security barrier that Israel is building between its eastern settlements and the Palestinians on the West Bank (*It works and it's not a WALL, it's only a fence*), and expose the Christians to liberal Israeli Jewish and Arab politicians and writers (*This is an open society, like yours*). The centerpiece was a visit to the Yad V'Shem Holocaust Museum (*We rest our case*).

The Christians responded with a trip to Bethlehem (*Israel occupies the birthplace of Jesus*), meetings with student activists at Bethlehem University (*The Zionists are stealing our water and trying to humiliate us into obedience*) and a man whose house has been demolished three times (*When humiliation fails, the Israelis use brute force*); and offered a Palestinian-eye view of the settlements (*Colonialism, pure and simple*). For their pièce de resistance the mainliners scheduled a visit to the Sabeel Center, where they introduced the Jews to Naim Ateek (*Here is a man who can refute all the propaganda your narrative is based on*).

The mission was, by all accounts, a civil affair. Both sides strained to demonstrate good manners and sensitivity. The liberal Jews conceded that the Palestinians had many grievances (and groused among themselves that they didn't need liberal Christians to instruct them that Israel has its flaws; why, they themselves had been criticizing Israel for years). The Christians conceded that the Jews, too, had a right to a state (even if it would be better

for everyone if it hadn't been created). The group issued a statement calling for a two-state solution, and everyone yawned. Israel
and the Palestinian Authority had long since adopted similar positions.

The Jews came back from this mission convinced they had won
the argument. "The ah-ha moment for the Christians came at Yad
V'Shem," said Ethan Felson, assistant director of the Jewish Council for Public Affairs. "We met with a professor from Hebrew University who described how Nazi propaganda and the *Protocols of the
Elders of Zion* permeate the Arab media. Seeing, in the post-
Holocaust era, that Arabs still feel almost like Nazis about the
Jews helped our Christian colleagues understand that we are still
vulnerable."

Felson pointed to the meeting with Naim Ateek as another dra-
matic, possibly mind-changing event. "During the trip we spent
the whole time talking among ourselves about how it isn't helpful
to deny each other's narratives," he recalled. "And then Ateek
stands up and says that Israel has no right to exist and it should
be located in Munich."

Canon Brian Grieves scored the trip differently. "I didn't learn
anything new about the Israeli perspective," he told me shortly
after returning to the United States. "Hopefully, our Jewish colleagues saw things that were sobering to them."

Grieves, who was born in London and educated at the University of Hawaii, described the Jewish part of the itinerary as a
comedy of errors. "They brought in an Israeli Palestinian journalist from the *Jerusalem Post.* We agreed with his assessment of the
Palestinian leadership, but then he began describing how he, as
an Israeli Arab, is a second-class citizen in his own country. I don't
think that's a message my Jewish colleagues wanted discussed."

As for the Holocaust, Grieves allowed that he had been very
much impressed by the recent architectural redesign of the Yad

V'Shem Museum. "The Palestinians need a Yad V'Shem too," he said.

Grieves returned from Israel under the impression that no gaps had been closed. "I don't think we and our Jewish colleagues can have the kind of deep relationship we both want until the Israeli-Palestinian conflict is resolved," he said.

Three months after the trip, in January 2006, that goal grew most distant when the Palestinians held an election and chose a Hamas government. Hamas adamantly opposes the two-state solution that the Christian-Jewish pilgrims had called for, a fact that didn't seem to change many minds on the Christian side. Brian Grieves and his colleagues chose to interpret the Hamas victory as simply a protest against the corruption of the previous PLO regime. Grieves told me that Israeli policies and behavior had driven the Palestinians into the arms of Hamas. He conceded that the Islamic fundamentalist doctrines of Hamas might make life harder for his Christian brethren in the Holy Land, but politics, in this case, would trump religious solidarity.

But the Hamas victory made Palestinian solidarity a much tougher sell in the pews of the mainline churches. Liberal Protestants may not be Zionists in the same way as evangelicals but, like most Americans—especially since 9/11—Israel is more to their taste than its radical Muslim enemies.

The Jewish establishment was aware of this, of course.

"We always knew that in a down-and-dirty vote on supporting Israel, we would win in almost every church in the country," Elcott told me. The establishment Jews had hoped that a trip to Israel might change the hearts and minds of the anti-Zionist activists, but, it turned out, they hadn't counted on it. In the autumn of 2004, the Jewish establishment across the country undertook a covert, grassroots campaign to defeat the divestment movement. "You start talking about not doing business with

Jews, there's an echo of the Nuremberg Laws in a strange way," says Jerry Benjamin, one of America's best-known Jewish demographers. "We explained that to local liberal Christian ministers and laypeople around the country and a lot of them understood it."

Suddenly, in 2006, the anti-Zionist wing of the mainstream denominations found itself under attack in its own churches. One by one, their national denominational bodies began backing away from the Israel–South Africa equation (not to mention Grieves's implicit Israel-Nazi comparison). The liberation theology activists didn't like this one bit. "I've raised this issue with our Jewish counterparts," I was told by Reverend Jay Rock, coordinator of interfaith relations for the Presbyterian Church (USA). "I don't think our interfaith trip to Israel changed opinions very much, but I can tell you that the [Jewish] tactic of talking directly to our people has. It has been very successful in getting them to think about this in a pro-Israeli way."

For his part, Elcott was unrepentant about this Jewish assault on the mainstream church. "Churches aren't isolated islands anymore," Elcott told me. "What happens in one affects everybody. In America we have the right and maybe the obligation to try to influence each other's thinking—even on matters of theology."

SEVEN

A FLY ON THE WAILING WALL

In December of 2005 I went on a Christian pilgrimage of my own to the Holy Land. My companions were thirty evangelicals from around the United States. None needed to be convinced of any Israeli narrative. They had the Bible, and that was enough.

We met at a small hotel in Jerusalem. The hotel was packed, the entire city was bustling. In the previous five years of intifada, tourists—one of the economic mainstays of the capital—had been rare. During the worst period of bombings, I once breakfasted at the famous King David Hotel and found myself sharing the massive dining room with only one other guest, the American mediator, General Anthony Zinni.

During the intifada, almost the only tourists in Jerusalem had been evangelical Christians. One year, on the holiday of Sukkot, I watched them march through the Old City of Jerusalem, surrounded by police and soldiers. A thin crowd of Israelis stood along the route and applauded. A pilgrim handed a piece of hard candy to a small boy wearing a skullcap. "Thank you," his father told the American in English. To the boy he said, in Hebrew, "Throw that in the street." The pious Jews of Jerusalem welcome the support of Christians, but that doesn't mean their candy is kosher.

• • •

STILL, THE ISRAELI-CHRISTIAN connection isn't controversial in Israel. Some Israeli hard-line leftists object to evangelicals because evangelicals are so pro-American. Some far-right rabbis oppose them as proselytizers in Zionist clothing. But mainstream Israelis, left and right, are far too pragmatic for such ideological or pietistic scruples. This is especially true in the tourist industry, where evangelicals are seen as little less than saviors.

"When I started out in this business ten years ago, I naturally concentrated on Jewish groups," said Mark, our Jerusalem-based tour guide who was born and raised in Montreal. "But the intifada taught us something. The future of tourism is Christian. American Jews will still come in the summertime, but that's going to be the icing on the cake. The cake is Christian Zionists, and that's just going to grow."

Mark was the leader of our group, along with travel agent Madeline Cohen, a former Israeli, now living in Chicago, who specializes in Christian tourism. She had put together this group for Yechiel Eckstein's International Fellowship of Christians and Jews. It was a random assortment of evangelicals from around the United States, people who had been strangers to one another until they met at the Toronto Airport en route to Israel. A few had never been outside the United States before. When they came down to dinner at the hotel dining room that first night, they wore looks of disoriented jet lag.

"You probably saw more Jews today riding through Jerusalem on the way to the hotel than you've seen in your life," I said to a lanky young woman from a small town in Montana.

She laughed. "I saw more Jews in the *airport*," she said. "I can't recall ever seeing *any* Jews before."

Ours was a diverse group, young and old, black and white, even a Roman Catholic. It included a retired naval commander with an interest in Zionist military history; an evangelist from Boston who once made national headlines for alleged child abuse; a Jamaican nurse from White Plains who had been inspired to visit Israel by Jewish urologists; an intense, mystical woman who installed airplane bathrooms at a Boeing plant in Seattle; a lady theologian with the gift of speaking in tongues; and a black woman from Atlanta who giggled continuously, made a modest living taking care of old people, and tithed her salary to Israel.

At dinner I sat across from a man who bore a striking resemblance to Steve McQueen. He introduced himself as Catfish but was vague about his business and residence. "Lately I've been living in Port Saint Lucie, Florida," he said.

I searched my memory for Port Saint Lucie small talk. I had just written an article on fifties rock and roll, and this piece of trivia surfaced. "Carl Gardner, the former lead singer of the Coasters, lives in Port St. Lucie."

"Is that right? I heard Dickie Dale lived around there too, for a while, but I never saw him," said Catfish.

George Mamo, a Christian lay preacher and official of the IFCJ, called the group to order. Mamo is a quiet, bearded man, a former Catholic who once worked for Winrock Confidential. He asked people to introduce themselves and say why they had come. An ex-cop from a small town near Los Angeles said that he'd been inspired by attending the bar mitzvah of his commanding officer's son. A woman from Arkansas said she'd been motivated by God's commandment to bless Israel. A black woman from Illinois said she was on a roots trip: "This land belongs to my people, too," she said. "Africa is home to us. So is Israel."

"I'm here because I want to learn more and know more," said Beth Jones, a pretty blonde in her forties who still looks like the captain of the cheerleader squad. She and her husband are co-pastors of a church in Kalamazoo, Michigan. She also writes books of popular Bible commentary and an advice column in the local newspaper. Her mother, who bears a striking resemblance to Lauren Bacall, sat next to her. "I'm here because my son-in-law blessed me with a trip," the mom said in a cigarette-inflected baritone.

I leaned over to Pastor Jerry Clark, another IFCJ staffer.

"What's that mean?" I asked. "That her son-in-law paid for the trip?"

Clark nodded. "I see you're starting to speak Christian," he said approvingly.

George Mamo presented me to the group as a writer who would be accompanying them. "I'm an Israeli Jew," I told them. "But in the next nine days I want to see Israel and Jews through Christian eyes."

I made it clear that no one should feel obliged to talk to me, but most of them did. They had personal stories to relate. A few may have looked upon me as conversion material but nobody brought it up. They were evangelical Christians, but they were also Americans who had been taught good manners.

Some, I knew, were suspicious of me and my motives. Born-again Christians are usually ridiculed by secular writers. Linda, the theologian, was especially alive to this possibility, and made me her project. "It's easy to mock some of these flamboyant television evangelists," she said. "They embarrass us too sometimes with their outrageous behavior. But I want you to understand that we're not all fakes or religious nuts. There is an intellectually and spiritually serious side to evangelical Christianity. I hope you see that, too."

Before the trip, the IFCJ sent out an information package with a list of things to pack: jeans, T-shirts, bathing suits, suntan lotion, sports clothes. There was nothing on the list that couldn't be bought at Wal-Mart. Say what you like about evangelical Christianity, it's the only fundamentalist religion I know that doesn't require uniforms and special equipment.

In fact, during my travels through evangelical America I had noticed that a lot of younger pastors have wives who go to church dressed like nightclub singers. Often the ministers openly brag to their congregations about their wives' beauty and glamour. There is more than a little sex in the evangelical appeal. My fellow pilgrims certainly weren't naive or inexperienced—quite the opposite, as I discovered during our trip.

A CHRISTIAN TOUR of Israel is, for an Israeli, an excursion into a different country. Contemporary Israel is of almost no interest to the pilgrims. During the entire trip I never saw anyone reading the *Jerusalem Post* or any other newspaper. There was almost no discussion of Big Issues. It was a given that everyone was pro-Israeli. No one displayed any interest at all in the Palestinian "narrative." The group even skipped the West Bank town of Bethlehem.

A couple of days into the trip, Palestinian terrorists launched a suicide attack on a shopping mall in Netanya, killing five and wounding dozens more. No one seemed concerned by this. The day after the bombing we passed Netanya on the way to the Galilee. Word spread through the bus, and a few people looked curiously out the window, but most just ignored the whole thing. I couldn't tell if such calm was a sign of faith or obliviousness.

•   •   •

WE BEGAN OUR tour of Jerusalem on the Mount of Olives, from which you can see the gleaming gold dome of the mosque that stands on the site of the First and Second Temples. Mark gave a dry account of the history of the place and a description of the mosque.

"The so-called mosque," one of the women said, and the others murmured approval. "These Muslims don't belong here."

"Why not move them to Jordan?" asked Catfish.

"Heck, the Jordanians don't want 'em," said Texas Jack, the retired lieutenant commander. He was a great admirer of Prime Minister Ariel Sharon, who, just a few days earlier, had left the hard-line Likud to form Kadima, a centrist party. Jack was all right with this move to the middle, which he regarded as tactical, but it didn't alter his own hawkish views. "I was in Saudi Arabia for a year and a half, got a pot of money, and left," he said. "There's nothing about the place I like. They settle everything with violence. They don't even have third-party insurance because if you get hit by somebody in a car, you're supposed to take revenge by hitting them back or something."

"Will the Temple ever be rebuilt?" asked the mom from Kalamazoo in her Lauren Bacall voice.

Mark was ready for the question evangelical groups always ask. "Most Orthodox Jews don't believe the Temple will be rebuilt until the Messiah comes," he said. In fact, pious Jews think it is sinful to so much as set foot on the Temple Mount for fear of inadvertently stepping into the Holy of Holies where only priests are supposed to trod. The majority of Israelis, however, are not expecting the Messiah; their interest in the Temple Mount tends to be symbolic and national, not religious.

One Israeli group that does keenly focus on the Temple Mount is the Shin Bet, Israel's internal security agency. It has long feared that Jewish fanatics may try to blow up the mosques and set off an international conflagration.

"The fanatics worry us," Mark said. "Sometimes my Christian friends say, 'Well, God *did* promise to reestablish the Temple.' And I say, 'Okay, but are you sure the time is now? If not, we could start World War III here.'"

From the Mount of Olives we went to the Garden of Gethsemane, where George Mamo read from the book of Matthew. "Jesus could have called down angels to save him but he didn't," said Mamo. "Because how could the scriptures be fulfilled if this [crucifixion] doesn't happen here in this way?" This is a cardinal tenet of evangelical Christianity as it is currently preached and understood. Jesus was not murdered by the Jews. He was a willing actor in a drama of his own creation, in which the crucifixion was a necessary element. The Jews, too, were actors, not free agents.

FROM GETHSEMANE WE went to a nearby religious supermarket run by George Nisan. He belongs to a small Assyrian Christian sect that still speaks Aramaic, and he greeted us by reciting the Lord's Prayer in the language of Jesus. It caused a stir—"Just like in *The Passion*," one woman said—but the evangelicals weren't interested in Nisan's Christian merchandise. They skipped the mother-of-pearl crèches, ornate wooden crosses, votary candles, and genuine crown-of-thorns made in Bethlehem and went straight for the Jewish stuff. One woman bought a shofar, a ceremonial ram's horn, so big she needed help carrying it to the bus.

Linda the theologian, my intellectual minder, explained: "There's a lot of curiosity because some people on this trip have never met a Jew before," she said. "This is a new experience for them. I grew up Swedish Lutheran, in Boston, and went to U Mass.

I've known Jews. And I've known anti-Semites, too. I had a Catholic friend who didn't like Jews. But when she became an evangelical Christian she prayed and prayed for an understanding of the Jewish people. Today, she's a member of the International Fellowship of Christians and Jews."

Linda saw the threat of Christian anti-Semitism emanating largely from the theological left. "Replacement theology is taking hold even at some of the more liberal evangelical colleges," she said darkly. This doctrine teaches that when the Jews rejected Jesus they lost their status as God's Chosen People and were replaced by the Church. Replacement theology concerns Christian Zionists, who see it as the path to liberation theology. "Because of replacement theory, it's become politically correct on certain Christian campuses not to have a heart for Israel," said Linda.

MANY OF THE pilgrims were open not just to Jewish products and customs, but to other religious traditions. The lanky lady from Montana, for example, had worked for the Bureau of Indian Affairs and was highly sensitive to the needs of her Native American clients. "They like to keep evil spirits away by what they call smudging," she told me. "They do it by burning prairie grass, and I always kept some for them in my desk."

But ecumenism stopped at the doors of the Roman Catholic Church. Strangely, almost half the pilgrims were lapsed Catholics themselves, and many spoke of their previous denomination with anger and contempt. When the group went to the Galilee, it skipped Nazareth. Mark explained that evangelicals don't usually visit the hometown of Jesus because it is dominated by Catholic churches and shrines. When I asked the group's lone practicing

Catholic about this, he simply shrugged. If he had wanted to visit Catholic sites, he said, he would have taken a Catholic tour.

ON SATURDAY MORNING I ate breakfast with Pastor Don Cobble from Boston by way of Alabama. Throughout the meal he kept hopping up and greeting his fellow guests in foreign languages. Cobble is a compact, peppy man who has spent years doing missionary work around the world. He prides himself on his ability to tell, say, an Uzbek from an Armenian, and to greet each in the appropriate tongue. "A few words at least," he explained to me. "Something familiar. It opens hearts."

In 1994, Cobble and his family returned from overseas missionary work and moved to Woburn, Massachusetts. Cobble's son Judah was nine years old and rambunctious. One day he came home from school with poor marks for behavior, and Cobble spanked him with a belt.

Judah's teacher heard about this, and she alerted the authorities. Cobble got a visit from the Massachusetts Department of Social Services.

"I told them I had given him a light spanking, which is how you're supposed to punish your children according to the Bible," Cobble told me. "Spare the rod and spoil the child? But as soon as they heard the word 'Bible' they were off and running."

Cobble was issued an official warning. He responded by taking the Department of Social Services to court, charging them with trying to deny him his right to practice religion. He lost in Superior Court, appealed, and won 5–0 in the Massachusetts Supreme Court. One Justice recalled, with obvious nostalgia, that when *he* was a boy he got his spankings with a wooden switch.

"They paid my court costs," Cobble said. "I was on a bunch of

national TV shows. My name was cleared and I made my point—
the government doesn't have the right to punish you because you
want to raise your child according to Christian principles."

One of those principles is unquestioning love for the Chosen
People. To Cobble's regret, it has gone largely unrequited, at least
in Massachusetts.

"Last year I invited three hundred rabbis from the Boston area
to participate in my church's rally for Israel. I only got one response
and that was a polite no. The Jewish newspaper in Boston didn't
even want to print an ad until the Israeli consulate intervened."

The Israelis sent a diplomat, but the rally was pretty much boy-
cotted by the local Jews. "It was awful disappointing," recalled
Cobble. "Jews in Boston don't want anything to do with evangelical Christians. They think we're missionaries."

"Well, are you?"

"Some are," Cobble said, "but we're not. There's a caucus in
the Israeli Knesset that supports ties with us. A lot of the members
of the caucus are Orthodox. If they thought we were bent on conversion, they'd cut us off just like that."

He snapped his fingers so loud he caught the attention of a
group of mustachioed businessmen at the next table. He greeted
them in a guttural language and they smiled. "Ukrainians,"
Cobble said. "I met them last night. Very nice people." He paused,
reading my mind. "And they definitely aren't Jewish."

AFTER BREAKFAST THE group took a walk in the Old City of
Jerusalem. Going up the Via Dolorosa we passed a knot of young
Palestinian men sitting on the stoop of a building. "I hear on the
news fifty Americans killed in Iraq," one hollered at us from no
more than ten feet away, "I very happy about this." His friends

laughed and cast challenging looks at us, but the pilgrims kept moving. As we walked toward the Church of the Holy Sepulcher I could hear shopkeepers happily calling out to one another, in Arabic, "American soldiers killed in Iraq!" while they gestured for the tourists to enter their stores. None did.

The incident surprised me. Palestinians are not rude people; like other Arabs, they pride themselves on hospitality and good manners with strangers. The fact that they were now shouting insults at tourists was an index of how radicalized and furious they had become. A few months later, when I heard that Hamas had won the Palestinian election, I recalled those voices on the Via Dolorosa.

THAT AFTERNOON WE took communion at the Protestant Garden Tomb. By the time Protestant denominations got to the Holy Land, all the good ecclesiastical real estate had been snapped up by Roman Catholics, Greek Orthodox, and various Eastern denominations. Protestants had solved this shortage with Calvinist ingenuity, by declaring a series of alternative holy places.

The Protestant Garden Tomb, putatively the place where Christ had been buried and risen, is located across the street from the Damascus Gate of the Old City, next to a bus park. My fellow pilgrims sat on simple chairs, ate matzo instead of wafers, and drank tiny cups of wine symbolizing Jesus' blood. I was next to Catfish, who was barefoot—he made a habit of removing his leather sandals whenever he entered a sacred site—and he noticed me skipping the wine.

"It's not a religious thing," I said. "I just don't drink. I quit almost ten years ago."

"I quit back then too," said Catfish. "After a shooting incident. But sometimes I slip up. You never slip up?"

"Not so far," I said. "But you never know."

"Yeah, that's the truth," he said. "See, back then, around 1994? Man, I was a mess. Crack cocaine, heroin, booze—you name it—I was doin' it. And I sorta just got out of control. I had this woman? She and I quarreled all the time until this one time I just grabbed a shotgun and aimed it right at her head, and I was about to pull the trigger on her when I heard Jesus say: 'Don't do that!' I just raised that barrel up and blew a hole right through the ceiling, and I walked out on that relationship and didn't never turn around."

"That's when you were saved?"

Catfish gave me an even look. "Saved is a big word," he said. "I had a lot of problems back then. I never did have any money, for one thing. I don't think I ever cleared more than $18,000 a year installing air conditioners. Sometimes I'd make a little extra taking guys out into the swamp to hunt wild hogs. I taught 'em how to kill the animal with a knife and cut its head off. Redneck work.

"Then my daddy fell sick and I went up to where he was and tended to him. I figured he'd help me out eventually, but when he died my brother got his hands on the old man's money. I was mad. I told my sister I was gonna take my brother out in the woods and wasn't but one of us coming back."

"And then what?"

"Let's just say, if it wasn't for Jesus, my brother wouldn't be alive today. I'm a sinner and I know it, but I'm trying to be better. I still smoke and drink, but not like I did. I might have three or four shots before dinner, and maybe a couple afterward, but I quit when I get that buzz."

"Your church doesn't frown on drinking?"

"I don't belong to a church," Catfish said. "I'm a Christian man and I'm trying to do my best to find some spiritual peace. Church hasn't got anything to do with that."

DURING THE TRIP Catfish stayed mostly to himself, but somehow everybody in the group eventually heard his story. The men began referring to him as "Ole Catfish" and the ladies fell for him in a chaste way. "I believe that if he were alive back in the day of Jesus," Beth said, "he would have been chosen as a disciple."

Catfish wasn't the only one with a history. Almost everyone in this band of outwardly bland, cheerful Americans seemed to be struggling with epic inner demons. Nobody flaunted their sins, but if you asked personal questions people responded with an amazing directness.

A middle-aged teacher from Arizona named Tonya sat next to me on the bus from Jerusalem to the Galilee. Making conversation, I asked why she had come on the trip.

"I was born with a rare childhood illness," she confided immediately. "My life was saved by Jewish doctors. Obviously, I need to give something back. So here I am. I know a lot of Jews are suspicious of us, but if you look at our gospel, really, it's all about love. God is love."

"God is love" is a formulation so un-Jewish that I don't even know how to express it in Hebrew. I was thinking about that when she said, "But still, the church can be smothering. A lot of evangelicals preach that you should fear God. And if you don't, he'll squash you like a bug. A lot of people feel that way."

"A lot of Orthodox Jews feel that way too," I said, but she wasn't really listening. She said, "Among Christians we have an expression, 'We kill our own.' One sin can be perceived as enough to send you to hell."

"Sure, but can't you repent and get saved?"

Tonya stared out the window, collecting her thoughts, took a deep breath, and said, "When I was sixteen years old I got pregnant. I was in a Christian high school. And everybody turned their backs on me. I even *married* the boy, but it didn't matter. My own family ostracized me. One woman in my church gave me a baby shower present. One woman.

"My baby died at two and a half months. The Christian school took my classmates on an educational trip to the cemetery, to see the grave. 'The wages of sin is death' is what the teacher told them."

Tears were running down her face. "I think maybe it's getting better now," she said. "These end-times teachings have a lot of so-called Christian people scared, and that makes them a little nicer to each other. I hope they are. Despite what I've been through, I've got to believe that God is love."

I DIDN'T SEE many books on the trip, except for the Bible, but a surprising number of pilgrims were amateur writers. My favorite was Giggles, the woman from Atlanta who took care of old people. This was her second trip to Israel. One day she handed me a note she had composed: "A lot of ideas are founded by the devil when ideas are negative, such as hip-hopping, dead-beating, soul train–dancing, women not respecting men and men not respecting women."

"You writing from personal experience?" I asked, expecting a giggle. Instead she nodded solemnly, took back the paper, and folded it away. The devil was no laughing matter.

Christians profess to believe in sin, of course, but sins come in different guises. Mainstream Protestants tend to locate sin in the moral malfeasance of others—slaveholders, colonialists, capitalists, settlers, oil barons, and the Bush administration. Evangelicals look inward. The sins are theirs, personally owned and operated and, in a perverse way, cherished. After all, the bigger the sin, the bigger the salvation.

Nobody in our group wanted to be caught without a sinful past. Even pretty Beth Jones confessed to me that she was "wild" in high school. Bob, the ex-cop, confided that he had been "rough on the streets." And then there was Gayle, the woman with the star of David on her blouse who had bought the huge shofar from the Aramaic-speaking shopkeeper in Jerusalem. She had sharp features and a strong New England accent, and she had been eying me throughout the trip. Finally, coming down the Carmel mountain range, near the spot where the prophet Elijah smote the false priests of Baal, she got up her nerve and sat next to me. "I'd like to tell you my story," she said. "I've been through the muck and mire."

She looked commandingly at my notebook, which I dutifully opened. "Start with the facts," she said. "My dad was Jewish. My mom was a Protestant. His family never really accepted her, even though she converted to Judaism and kept a kosher home. There was bad blood. My father was in medical school, and he was beloved by his parents. They were very Orthodox and they couldn't believe he had married a shiksa.

"When I was a little girl my father ran away, just disappeared. And as I grew up, I was wild. Boys? Yeah, I was crazy for boys. And booze. You name it. I mean, I had no identity, no self-respect. Who was I? A Jew? My mother didn't practice Judaism after my father left. A Christian? She never took me to church. I was nothing. But even then, even when I was drinking and running wild, I knew there was a God.

"I yearned for my father. At nineteen I married a man because he looked like my father's picture. We had a son, but my husband beat me and abused me and we split up. I was in sin up to my eyeballs. Sin was my escape. I didn't care about anything really. We were on welfare. We lived in a slum. Then one day, a fire burned us out. A family took us in for a few days, but they didn't really want us, and they asked us to leave.

"I was out on the street with my son, and I had a visitation from the Lord. He said, 'Come unto me, just as you are.'

"It opened my eyes," she said, opening hers to demonstrate. "I went off welfare and walked with God."

Suddenly, things began to fall into place. Her Jewish grandparents died and she reconciled with her father's aunts. She met a fine Christian man, married him, and prospered. And then, after forty-three years, she found her father.

"He had become a Baptist minister and he was living in West Virginia with a wife I didn't care for and seven kids. Here we were, all those years later, reunited. That's why I can say that I truly walk with God. That's why I'm blessed to be able to give thousands of dollars to Israel. And that's why I wear this Jewish star, as a reminder of where I was and who I truly am."

ONE OF THE highlights of every pilgrimage is the chance to get baptized in the Jordan River. Israel has established a more or less official site (the Jordanians have a competing spot on the other bank). Next to it is a tourist complex run by Kibbutz Kinneret, whose Eastern European socialist-atheist founders would have been amazed by the vast gift store of Christian knickknacks being hawked by their grandchildren.

It was a chilly day, and not everyone wanted to get dunked in the cold river water. Only ten of the pilgrims, wearing bathing suits under rented white robes, went down to the baptismal pool. As they were taking their places, an Israeli guide called out to

Mark in Hebrew. "You got a priest with you? I have some people here who want to get baptized, but they don't have a priest." He gestured to a small group of men and women in colorful native robes. One couple wore baptismal gowns.

"Where are they from?" hollered Mark.

"Tahiti. Catholics. What are yours?"

"Evangelicals. You better check with yours that a Protestant minister is okay."

"It'll be fine, don't worry," said the other guide. "Just don't mention it."

George Mamo and Pastor Jerry performed the ceremony, holding each person by the arms and lowering him or her backward into the water. When the Tahitian couple's turn came, their friends sang a beautifully complex, presumably Catholic, anthem, accompanied by loud amens from our group. Then everyone dried off and went to the gift shop to buy souvenirs. As we were leaving, Don Cobble said good-bye in Tahitian.

ON THE WAY to our hotel in Tiberias, Linda the theologian sat with me. "I've always been uncomfortable with displays of religious emotion," she said quietly. "Perhaps it's my Scandinavian temperament. But you know, ever since I became an evangelical Christian I've been, well, uncomfortable I guess is the right word."

"Like John Kerry," I said. "Another New Englander who doesn't wear his religion on his sleeve."

Linda smiled. "He did say that, didn't he? Well, I can understand him. But, then, there are surprises. You can surprise yourself. I live in Florida now. During the last hurricane I was alone in the house, desperately trying to close the shutters. I realized that I had underestimated the sheer strength of the wind. I was frightened that the storm would blow the windows in. And suddenly, to my own great amazement, I found myself talking to Jesus. Talking in tongues."

"Really?"

"Yes. Does that shock you?"

"No," I lied. Linda was the voice of sophisticated academic evangelical Christianity, my partner in dispassion. Talking in tongues, a feature of charismatic Pentecostalism of the Pat Robertson variety, is considered eccentric and perhaps heretical by some fundamentalists. Many Baptists even regard it as a satanic practice.

"Actually, it's more a way of channeling spirituality than anything else," Linda said. "You don't intellectualize your prayers by verbalizing them, you simply allow them to flow through you, and they express themselves in a language you may not understand but that is consonant with your innermost feelings."

"Like a mantra?"

"Perhaps. I'm not certain that would be an exact analogy. Would you like to hear how it sounds?"

I nodded. I had heard people speaking in tongues in Pentecostal churches before—fervent semishouts and unintelligible grunts and moans. But Linda spoke in tongues as she spoke in English, softly and fluently, her quiet blue eyes focused on mine. She could have been telling me a story in Swedish. When she was finished she paused and looked at me evenly.

"Do you know what you just said?" I asked.

"Not in words, no. And not really emotionally this time, either. I just wanted you to hear how it sounds."

THERE WAS A health spa at our hotel in Tiberias and we all gravitated to it. It featured stationary bikes, an artificial waterfall, a swimming pool, and a hot tub, where I found myself sitting with Giggles, Beth, and her mother. Me and three born-again women, in modest bathing suits, sharing a soak.

Beth reminisced about hot tubs past, when she was one of the popular chicks in her Kalamazoo high school. Her mom recalled those days with a proud smile. She herself hadn't been an evangelical back then. In fact, she said, after her divorce there had been a time . . .

"I'm celibate," said Giggles suddenly, and giggled. The comment was unprompted but not inappropriate. During the trip I hadn't heard so much as a crude word or a suggestive remark, but sex, I realized, had been a constant undercurrent. Most of the personal stories began with confessions of wild youthful behavior, and no one, people emphasized, was ever really out of the grasp of evil. I had encouraged these reminiscences with my questions. Giggles was letting me know she was aware that Satan comes in many forms, maybe even a bearded Jew in a Galilee hot tub.

NEXT DAY AT lunch, in a fish restaurant on the eastern bank of the Sea of Galilee, I sat with Linda, Pastor Beth and her mother, and Catfish.

"Zev and I discussed speaking in tongues yesterday," said Linda in the tone of a teacher introducing a seminar topic. The floor was now open for discussion.

"Never happened to me," said Catfish.

Beth said, "I speak in tongues. Not necessarily in church on Sunday, we don't have that kind of congregation. But sometimes— do you know if the word *shem* has a meaning?"

"It's one of the ways to refer to God in Hebrew," I said.

"I knew it! When I was in college I started to hear three words in my head. Does *kadeesh* mean anything? Or *hodiyah*?"

"*Kadeesh* has to do with holiness," I said. "*Hodiyah* is thanksgiving."

"I knew it, I just knew it!" said Beth. "Those words kept coming to my mind and they were the words I used when I first spoke in tongues!"

I must have looked skeptical because she said, "Not everything can be explained logically. I mean, have you heard about Reverend Kim Clements from South Africa? He prophesized the flood in New Orleans. And he's not a whacko. I mean, some Baptists think prophecy is weirdness, but the proof is in the pudding."

"There's been a lot of talk lately about a Lutheran minister in Indonesia who's had a lot of success raising the dead," said Beth's mom in her Bacall baritone.

"I've heard that," said Linda. "He's said to be a very straightforward person. I also heard a story about a man in Africa whose brother died, he'd been dead for two days, and there was a preacher nearby who could supposedly raise the dead. So the man put his brother on the back of a flatbed truck and drove him to the preacher. The preacher said the man should put his hands on his brother's ill place, and when he did, the brother came back to life."

"Well," I said. I had made it a practice not to argue with anyone during this trip or anywhere else during my time with evangelicals. I wanted to know what *they* thought, not convince them of anything. But this seemed a bit much. Linda saw skepticism and, to buttress her story, said, "That preacher lives in Florida now."

There was a long silence. Then Catfish said, "I got to get that guy's name."

"You'd think that a man like that would be famous," I said.

Linda fixed me with her mild blue eyes and said, "People are afraid of this subject. They simply don't *want* to know. I mean, I can see that it's hard to believe, but there are just so many testimonies."

MIGDAL HAEMEK IS a rundown little town in the Galilee, a place settled by successive waves of Jewish immigrants and lived in by those too poor or too lazy to move someplace better. It is also the home of Yitzhak Grossman, an Orthodox rabbi who runs a town within the town for six thousand Israeli orphans and unwanted children. The Migdal Or Boys and Girls Village is a major recipient of evangelical contributions, and we visited to see how the money was being spent.

Grossman is a tall, thin, imposing figure with a white beard and a piercing gaze. Dressed in his long black coat and broad-brimmed black hat, he looked like a Jewish Wyatt Earp. In his younger days he earned fame as the "disco rabbi," one of the few Israeli clerics willing to venture into forbidden secular night-spots to make contact with kids. Eventually he broadened his outreach to prisoners. Now, a lot of his rehabilitated former charges belong to his eight-hundred-member staff, which includes teachers, councilors, coaches, adoptive parents, and even a full-time marital matchmaker.

Before we arrived, Mark had briefed the group on protocol, warning the women not to touch Rabbi Grossman physically. "It's just not done," he explained. "It's a matter of female impurity, menstrual and so forth."

"When we visited Africa, the women had to wrap their legs for some of the tribal leaders," said the airline plumber.

Rabbi Grossman speaks English with a thick accent, in which boys are *boy-es* and girls *girlies*. The pilgrims listened to him intently, and Grossman was perfectly at home with them. Unlike many of his ultra-pious colleagues, he knows the evangelical world well and has appeared on TV with John Hagee, Pat Robertson, and other televangelists.

As we moved around Migdal Or we were welcomed with songs and ceremonies. Little kids in skullcaps bowed as they crossed Grossman's path. Teenagers paused for a word with him, sometimes kissing his hand. He led us through the village for more than an hour, winding up in the communal dining room for lunch and entertainment.

The fare was institutional and strictly kosher—overcooked chicken and soggy side dishes. Beth, sitting nearby, wondered if she could get a glass of milk. "Not here," I said.

"Don't Jews drink milk?"

"Not with meat."

"Why not?"

I couldn't resist. "It's forbidden," I told her solemnly. "In the Bible."

After lunch Rabbi Grossman brought in the boys' choir, a dozen or so preteens in matching vest-and-slack outfits, microphone headsets over their black silk yarmulkes. Music blared from large speakers and the boys began singing and moving, choreographed as the Jackson 5, Hebrew psalms set to a disco beat. The pilgrims clapped along with enthusiasm as Grossman looked on, beaming.

The dining hall and the entire campus are strewn with photos of Rabbi Grossman posing with the great Orthodox rabbis of Israel. Many of these rabbis have never met a Christian in their lives and don't want to. Grossman, who has turned down the job of chief rabbi, provides the evangelicals with an important religious and political imprimatur in Israel. If these Christians are kosher enough for him, they are sufficiently kosher for a whole lot of other rabbis with short budgets and high aspirations.

On the way back to the bus Jack, the lone Catholic, approached Rabbi Grossman. "Will you bless me, Rabbi?" he said.

Grossman smiled and placed his hands on Jack's head. "Help the boyes and the girlies and you will be blessed," he said.

ON THE WAY to the Mount of Beatitudes I fell into a discussion with several of the women about a previously taboo subject—my ultimate destination. I raised the issue myself, bluntly. "Do you think I'm going to hell?" I asked.

The women looked at one another and bit their lips. Finally Pastor Beth said that she hoped everyone would ultimately go to heaven.

"Even if they don't accept Jesus?"

Again they exchanged glances. They had an American horror of being rude but they couldn't lie. "We don't *want* you to go to hell," Linda said in her kindly way. "It's not up to us, it's up to God. But here on earth we truly love you. Why not judge us by our fruits?"

"Because a lot of Christian fruits have been bitter," I said. "The Crusades, the Inquisition . . ."

Beth said, "But it's different now. That's all changed." Evangelicals don't deny history. Some believe they need to atone for it. But that isn't their primary motive in loving Jews and supporting Israel. They believe the Jews are God's people. They can't change that any more than they can change the rest of God's plan.

That evening at dusk we took a boat ride on the Sea of Galilee aboard the model of a fishing ship from the time of Jesus. The sun was setting as we sailed toward Tiberias. The captain, a rough-looking Israeli in a T-shirt and jeans, flipped on a sound system especially programmed for evangelicals, and Mahalia Jackson's voice boomed across the water: "He's got the whole world in his hands."

"Come on, everybody, clap your hands!" shouted Madeline Cohen, our peppery Israeli travel agent. Some of the women rose and began doing an approximation of the hora while the men watched bashfully.

"Something faster," Madeline called out to the captain in Hebrew. "They want to dance."

"Okay, okay," the captain said and switched to Israeli Euro-pop dance tunes.

"Dance, dance!" yelled Madeline Cohen.

Catfish came up to me. "I'm just a dumb redneck, I know that, but I saw the sun come up over the sea this morning and a little poem came to me, about the love of God. Can I read it to you?"

I nodded. He took a neatly folded sheet of paper from his shirt pocket and began to recite:

As I came to the motherland
My heart was hard and sad.
But as I walked where Jesus walked
I started to understand
Why people have always fought
For this beautiful and wonderful land.

And now I find myself not sleeping at night
Now wondering about my sins

So from this land of the holy
I got down on my knees
To ask the good lord for forgiveness
Of my wicked and evil deeds

And now I found myself crying
As the lord was crying for this land.
And so another day has come and gone
As I travel through this land.

I found my heart happy
As I was praising this holy land.

And now my journey is ending
As my heart is changing again
I found myself grieving
For this great and holy land.

But as I make this promise
That I will return again
And those who hear these words
May we meet in peace
In this wonderful and holy land.

A few months after the trip, I spoke with Catfish on the phone. He was in Port Lucie, still installing air conditioners, but he had a new avocation. "I've set up a foundation," he said. "I'm calling it the Sea of Galilee Foundation. I'm putting up a website and I'm going to sell the picture I took of the sun going up over the Galilee and copies of my poem. I'll keep ten percent, and the rest goes to Rabbi Grossman's orphans and an orphanage here in America. The way I figure it, even if I only keep ten percent? It's like Jesus is letting me win the lottery."

PART TWO

IS IT GOOD FOR THE JEWS?

EIGHT

THE KINGDOM GUY

I heard rumors about Yechiel Eckstein before I met him. Word reached New York that a Chicago rabbi—an *Orthodox* rabbi—had become a televangelist. He was, it was said, taking in millions of dollars from evangelical Christians. This was startling. Even more amazing, he was said to be giving the money away to Jewish charities.

Ever since my father had forced me to cut the grass of the local rabbi for free, I have regarded people of the cloth as *schnorrers*—expert beggars—and nothing I saw of the political divines in Israel ever disabused me of that idea. Now here was a rabbi who supposedly not only pushed his own lawn mower but carried a magical checkbook. This I had to see for myself.

Our first meeting, in March 2004, was in Manhattan, over lunch. I let Eckstein pick the place, which was a mistake. It is a rule of thumb never to eat in a restaurant where the kosher certificate is bigger than the menu. But we hit it off despite the execrable pizza. I wrote a column about Eckstein in the New York *Daily News,* and began following his activities. Not exactly publicity-averse, Eckstein invited me to visit him in Chicago at the headquarters of his International Fellowship of Christians and Jews. In the spring of 2005, I took him up on the offer, especially after he volunteered to throw in a road trip to Indiana.

"THIS GUY IS a kingdom guy," said Pastor Steve Munsey, pointing his finger at Rabbi Eckstein. We were sitting in the Green Room of the Family Christian Center in Munster, Indiana, about forty minutes from Chicago. It was between Sunday morning services, and Pastor Steve was taking a break, kicking back to welcome his guest. "What do I mean by kingdom guy? Like a godfather in the mafia. It's a term of respect."

Eckstein accepted the compliment with a bland smile and sipped his coffee; Family Christian Center, we had already been informed by Associate Pastor David Jordan Allen, is the only church in the United States that has its own Starbucks. Eckstein has spent a lifetime in Pentecostal churches, but rarely had he seen one this grand. The FCC boasted a 3,000-seat auditorium and a pulpit adorned by a theatrical set of biblical Jerusalem complete with Golgotha's Hill and, in the words of Pastor Steve, "a very lifelike cave depicting the tomb where Jesus was lain."

A lanky deacon came over to shake Eckstein's hand and said, "It's a thrill to meet a man like you." Eckstein smiled again. The deacon was reputed to be one of the biggest steel contractors in the country. Devout Christian laymen like him have built Eckstein an empire. "I'm with Israel and the Jewish people all the way."

"I support Israel in every way possible," said Pastor Steve, regaining control of the conversation. "For example, I make it a point to buy my clothes from Jews." A small, compact man of fifty, he was wearing jeans and a battered sport jacket, an outfit that made it impossible to assess the monetary value of this sartorial contribution. Pastor Steve was dressed with such ostentatious informality because he planned to ride his customized Harley motorcycle onto the pulpit that morning. The bike, he explained, is named "The Passion" and it has a crown of thorns painted on the rear fender.

The door opened and Bishop Frank Munsey walked in. He is Pastor Steve's father. Bishop Munsey founded the Family Christian Center fifty years ago, and then passed it along to his son. Someday Pastor Steve will turn it over to his own son, Pastor Kent. "We call it Levitical succession," Associate Pastor Allen explained. If he felt frustrated by the glass ceiling of nepotism, he gave no sign of it.

Pastor Steve made the introductions. "Meet Rabbi Einstein," he said to his father. "You've seen him on TV. He's the head of the International Fellowship of Jews and Christians."

"You from the Jewish side or the Christian side?" asked the elderly bishop in a throaty voice. Lately he had been spending a good deal of time in Bulgaria, where his church runs a still unlicensed mission school.

"Jewish," said Eckstein, touching his small black skullcap. He didn't bother correcting Pastor Steve's mangled introduction.

The bishop's face lit up. Evidently he considered this a grand stroke of luck. For some reason, he was under the impression that Jews govern Bulgaria and were, for motives of their own, withholding accreditation from his school. Now, here was a Jewish rabbi sitting right in the Green Room. "I'd like to ask you a favor," he said, handing Eckstein a card. "Maybe you can get somewhere with these Bulgarians."

Eckstein took the card and placed it in his pocket. Help the born-again Christians of Bulgaria? Sure, why not. You never know what opportunities might present themselves.

•   •   •

SINCE HE BEGAN his ministry to the gentiles in 1980, Yechiel Eckstein has traveled to China to liberate persecuted preachers, hiked through Ethiopia and Siberia in search of endangered Jews, advised prime ministers in Jerusalem, and fellowshipped with evangelical Republicans at the White House. His immediate plans included transporting the biblical "lost tribe" of Manasseh from northeast India to the Holy Land, launching a Spanish-language campaign among the Pentecostals of Latin America, preaching in several Asian churches, and, maybe, recording some sacred hymns with Debbie Boone. And, as Eckstein himself would say, God only knew what would come after that.

All this hyperactivity is financed by the contributions of evangelical Christians. In the last eight years alone, approximately half a million born-again donors have sent Eckstein about a quarter of a billion dollars for Jewish causes of his personal choosing. No rabbi since Jesus has commanded this kind of gentile following. None today has his financial clout.

The IFCJ is now ranked among America's top four hundred charities by the *Chronicle of Philanthropy*. The Israeli newspaper *Ha'aretz* lists it as Israel's second largest charitable foundation. All this money has made Eckstein a much sought after fellow in certain Jewish circles—and a pariah in others.

Some of Eckstein's fellow Orthodox rabbis have tried to excommunicate him. Liberal Jews denounce his friendship with evangelicals as cultural and political treason. Even those who applaud Eckstein's philanthropies are sometimes dubious about what he calls his "ministry."

ECKSTEIN DIDN'T START out to be controversial. The son of an Orthodox rabbi in Ottawa, Canada, he got his own rabbinical ordination from Yeshiva University and joined the staff of the Anti-Defamation League (ADL). In those early days he was the model of a young mainstream Jewish organization man.

In 1977, American Nazis threatened to stage a march in Skokie, Illinois, a Chicago suburb with a large population of Holocaust survivors. The ADL sent Eckstein from New York to help the local community organize and round up Christian support. What he found surprised him. Jesse Jackson was headquartered in Chicago but, unlike his mentor, Martin Luther King Jr., who was always attentive to Jewish causes, Jackson had little interest. White Protestant mainstream churches were apathetic at best. The American Civil Liberties Union actually supported the First Amendment rights of the Nazis to march. Eckstein was surprised to find that evangelicals, more than any other group, were prepared to stand with the Jews of Skokie.

He went back to New York with this news like Marco Polo returning from China. There were conservative Christians in the heartland who took the Bible literally and believed the Jews were God's Chosen People. Not only that, they wanted to be friends. Eckstein saw this as a vast reservoir of support, an untapped resource for Israel, Soviet Jewry, and other causes, but his report was greeted in New York with incredulity. Few ADL leaders had actually met an evangelical. As far as they were concerned, born-again Christians were KKK night riders, toothless fiddlers, and flat-earth troglodytes. They ordered Eckstein to return to Chicago and commune with some respectable Episcopalians.

In 1980, the head of the Southern Baptist Convention, Reverend Bailey Smith—who had come to office as the result of a conservative coup in the Southern Baptist denomination—publicly declared that God doesn't hear the prayers of Jews. The Jewish establishment went crazy. Here was proof, if more proof was needed, that Christian fundamentalist anti-Semitism was alive and well in the boondocks—always a worthwhile discovery for fund-raising as well as a boost to the communal sense of beleaguered solidarity.

Eckstein saw a different sort of opportunity. Smith, a small-town preacher from Oklahoma, had been shocked and mortified by the national publicity his remarks engendered, and he was more than eager to clear himself of any and all charges of bigotry. When the head of the Dallas office of the ADL, Mark Briskman, contacted Reverend Smith and suggested a trip to Israel, Smith readily agreed. And Eckstein decided to join them.

In Jerusalem, Smith got the royal treatment. Prime Minister Begin, who had lost eight straight national elections before winning office, had few illusions about the efficacy of Jewish prayer. He did, however, know the value of allies. Did Reverend Smith believe that the Bible had conferred title to the land of Israel on the Jews? Splendid! Begin put out word to make Smith's trip enjoyable.

Smith enjoyed, and he returned to his fellow Baptists loudly proclaiming the message of Genesis 12:3: "God will bless those who bless Israel and curse those who curse Israel." Around this time, Jerry Falwell, Pat Robertson, and other fundamentalist preachers were saying the same thing, but Smith was an organization man, head of the largest Protestant denomination in the country.

"That was the turning point," says Eckstein. "From that moment on, I had an open door to every Baptist church in America."

In 1981, Israel bombed the Iraqi nuclear reactor, sparking worldwide rage. Even the normally pro-Israel Reagan administration was officially critical (although the wink from the White House was practically audible). The *New York Times* was scandalized. Many American Jewish leaders ran for cover.

But the evangelicals were not merely supportive, they were en-

thusiastic. When Begin called Falwell on the day after the bombing to ask for his help marshaling conservative opinion, Falwell
congratulated the Israeli prime minister for "putting one right
down the smokestack" and promised to stand by Israel all the
way.

WHEN YECHIEL ECKSTEIN brought all this to the attention of
the ADL home office, he was again rebuffed as a simpleton and a
nudnik. If Menachem Begin wanted to cozy up to Bailey Smith
and Jerry Falwell and other such hick undesirables, that was Begin's problem. Begin was an embarrassment anyway.

But Eckstein knew what he knew. He quit the ADL and tried,
unsuccessfully, to interest some other mainstream Jewish group in
establishing relations with the Christian fundamentalists. There
were no takers. Eckstein didn't even bother reaching out to his
fellow Orthodox rabbis, many of whom considered (and still consider) even setting foot in a Christian church to be a grave sin.

Instead, Eckstein went back to Chicago and opened his own
organization, which he grandly dubbed the International Fellowship of Christians and Jews. He had no salary, no health plan, no
insurance, and a pregnant wife. By day he made a little money as
a part-time congregational rabbi. In off-hours he toured the
country, going from church to church preaching a gospel of
Jewish-Christian common interest and solidarity.

By this time, the American Jewish community had been very
thoroughly *schnorred* by an army of enterprising fund-raisers. But
Eckstein found himself in virgin territory. Evangelicals badly
wanted to express their love for Jews and Israel in a personal way.
It was his insight that nothing is more personal than a personal
check.

• • •

"ASK AND IT shall be given," says Matthew 7:7. "Knock and it shall be opened unto you." In those first years of knocking, Eckstein barely made ends meet. He got some money from plate-passing Christians on Sunday mornings, and a little more from Jews—mostly political activists who were waking up to the nascent political power of the evangelical vote. "I don't know what you're doing, and I don't know if I like what you're doing," a Democratic Jewish philanthropist from Chicago told him, "but I'll give you a thousand bucks just in case."

Eckstein's next big breakthrough came in 1993. The gates of the former Soviet Union were open and tens of thousands of poor Jews wanted to emigrate to Israel. He knew that the ingathering of Jewish exiles resonated with evangelicals as biblical prophecy. With $25,000, he recorded his first TV infomercial. *On the Wings of Eagles* was hosted pro bono by Pat Boone, who delivered a message from Isaiah 49:22: "I will beckon to the Gentiles—they will bring your sons in their arms and carry your daughters on their shoulders." The show aired throughout the United States on Christian TV stations and the money began flowing in. "When I told Pat Robertson how much people were sending, he thought I was totally inflating the numbers," Eckstein recalls. In all, the infomercial ran for eighteen months and raised millions. Yechiel Eckstein was on his way.

THE AUDITORIUM OF the Family Christian Center was packed for the second service. The congregation, like most evangelical megachurches these days, was racially mixed. Munster, Indiana, is a white, semirural area, but the church aggressively recruits blacks in nearby Gary. Pastor Steve and his minister of music are white, but the choir is mostly black, and it started things off with a rousing rendition of "God Bless America" while giant screens projected action scenes of U.S. troops in Iraq.

Assistant Pastor Allen sat with me in the front pew and provided a running commentary. According to him, roughly 70 percent of the members of the Family Christian Center are Republicans. "A lot of the African Americans came as Democrats, but some of them are turning Republican, too," he said. He seemed proud of the diverse makeup of the church, whose members included establishment figures like the local sheriff and the prosecutor, a club of bikers-for-Jesus, and even a Jewish convert who played Pontius Pilate in the recent Easter pageant.

The choir started singing "Amazing Grace" and Pastor Steve, who had been sitting nearby, rose to take the pulpit on foot (the Harley ride came later). As he passed by he leaned down and whispered to me, "I have a passion for healing. We have the highest rate of cancer healings in the nation in this church." He said it in the matter-of-fact tone of a guy bragging about his bowling average.

Pastor Steve, shaggy-haired as an aging hippie, is a salesman as well as a showman. That morning he offered his congregation a warranty on tithing. "If God doesn't pay you back, with increase, in ninety days, then I'll refund the money myself," he promised to serious applause.

Israeli flags appeared on the huge screens above the pulpit and Pastor Steve summoned his guest. "Yek-eel Epstein is a powerful giant," he proclaimed, butchering the name again with Midwestern aplomb. "He rates right up there. You've seen him on TV. He was a rabbi and he became a born-again Christian!"

Eckstein, sitting nearby, visibly blanched. For decades his Jewish critics have spread the slander that he is a closet Christian, a missionary out to steal Jewish souls for Jesus. A few years ago, four senior Orthodox rabbis convened a religious court of inquiry in New York to try him for the "crime" of "teaching Torah to gentiles." He was acquitted in a split decision, but it was one of the great humiliations of his life.

The verdict didn't end the muttering, either. As Eckstein has grown more powerful, he has attracted ever harsher criticism from parts of the Orthodox community whose good opinion he covets. Just a few days earlier, the *Jewish Observer*, house organ of the ultra-Orthodox Agudat Yisrael of America, had called his work "a curse." And now here he was, publicly getting introduced as a born-again Christian, with a writer sitting there in the front pew. "This has never happened to me before," he muttered to me, as he rose to applause. "I've got to do something."

Despite his consternation, Eckstein appeared perfectly composed as he took the pulpit. He has the physical presence of an Eagle Scout troop leader, tall, broad-shouldered, and friendly-faced. The black yarmulke he wears is intentionally unobtrusive. Sometimes when he is traveling, he replaces it with a baseball cap.

"Shalom," he called to the congregation in a lilting voice.

"Shalom," they replied tentatively.

"Come on, I can't hear you. Give me a Shalom they can hear all the way to Jerusalem!" The congregation responded with a high-energy "Shalom!" and Eckstein, who has the bland delivery of a Canadian folksinger, grinned at his successful foray into Pentecostal call-and-response.

Sunday services in megachurches like the Family Christian Center are tightly scripted. Giant or not, Eckstein got just five minutes on the pulpit (he'd get another ten at next service) and he began his remarks with damage control. "I'm a Jewish rabbi," he informed the puzzled congregation. "An *Orthodox* Jewish rabbi.

I believe in *a* Messiah, but I am an Orthodox *Jewish* rabbi." There was applause and Eckstein smiled again, relieved to have reestablished his kosher bona fides without insulting either Pastor Steve or Jesus.

Eckstein went on to thank the congregation for their support for Israel. He spoke not merely as a rabbi but as an official emissary of the Jewish state. Although Eckstein's office remains in Chicago, he officially moved to Israel and became a citizen in 1999. His Jerusalem branch has a staff of ten and hands out millions of dollars to Israeli charity projects, from mobile dental clinics to antiterror systems. Naturally, such largess has not gone unnoticed by Israeli politicians. Prime Minister Ariel Sharon appointed him an unofficial adviser. Sharon's political rival, Foreign Minister Sylvan Shalom, topped that by naming Eckstein official Israeli emissary to evangelicals of the United States, Latin America, Africa, Korea, and other places where Protestant fundamentalism is on the rise. When he spoke for Israel, it was with the authority of an ambassador.

There was a huge digital clock mounted on the face of the FCC's balcony, ruthlessly counting down time. Eckstein spoke about the challenges facing Israel and the Jewish people, citing a few biblical passages about God blessing those who bless the Jews. It was a corny performance, and the audience loved it.

At the stroke of five minutes, Pastor Steve reclaimed his pulpit with a grand gesture. "We're going to plant a seed today," he announced, handing Eckstein a check for $5,000. "Remember, when you bless the Jewish people, God blesses you. So I want you all to tell Rabbi Einstein, thank you, Rabbi!"

"Thank you, Rabbi!" they hollered, as Eckstein pocketed the donation.

•   •   •

"I HAD THEM at 'Shalom,'" Yechiel Eckstein said. We were on our way back to Chicago in a rented compact Chevy, Eckstein sprawled in the back, his assistant, Reverend Jerry Clark, at the wheel. Self-deprecating humor is one of the ways Eckstein struggles against the sin of pride.

Even Eckstein's severest Jewish critics admit that he has an unrivaled ability to reach conservative Christians, and many who once mocked or opposed him for relying on the kindness of strangers now want his help. Hadassah, the Zionist women's organization whose magazine once refused to run Eckstein's paid ads, now begs to do joint projects with him. A few years ago the chairman of the Jewish Agency, the international governing body of Zionism, declined to be photographed with Eckstein. Today Eckstein is a member of the Jewish Agency Board of Governors. Even colleagues in the Orthodox Rabbinical Council of America who once scorned him have seen the light. In 2004, despite a nasty protest by some influential rabbis, RCA invited Eckstein to address its annual meeting.

These erstwhile skeptics have not developed a sudden enthusiasm for evangelical Christianity. They want to know Eckstein's fund-raising secrets. Just that week he had attended a meeting of major Jewish philanthropies in Las Vegas, but he had adamantly refused to share his techniques or computer files.

"These evangelicals are pure," he said, gesturing through the back window as we drove through the fields of Indiana on the way back to Chicago. "I represent the Jewish people to them. And I know very well how cynical some of these Jewish fund-raisers are. They're just in it for the buck. I should let them manipulate evangelicals like that?"

This attitude has won Eckstein detractors among the leaders

of secular Jewish organizations. Some, like the executive director of the Anti-Defamation League, Abraham Foxman, accuse him of poor-mouthing. A few years ago, Foxman demonstratively walked out of a meeting in which Eckstein was getting an award. He accused Eckstein of "selling the dignity of the Jewish people" by pandering to Christians. "We're not a poor people. What [Eckstein's] doing is perverse," Foxman told the *Jerusalem Report*.

YECHIEL ECKSTEIN HAS a genuine belief in the basic goodness of evangelicals. A typical headline in one of his solicitations reads: "Needy Jews Discovered in the Arctic Region." He runs campaigns to save the Russian Jews from "the scourge of anti-Semitism," as if the Communists were still in power, and calls for assistance to "elderly people living in dire need across the Holy Land," as though Israel weren't a modern welfare state. But to Eckstein, this misses the point. "I consider what I do more than fund-raising," he says. "It's a ministry. Christians have a need to give."

"Jews contribute to Jewish causes out of communal obligation," he told me. "They say, 'Send me a letter and a tax deduction statement and I'll give you something. If I have a good year I'll up it by five or ten percent next time.' Evangelical Christians find that abhorrent. They don't give out of responsibility. They give because the Lord told them to give. They're *moved* to do it."

Eckstein has dozens of stories to illustrate the point. "We used to get a check every month from a woman in Detroit, something like $26.18. She turned out to be [billionaire philanthropist] Max Fisher's maid. There's a woman in Georgia who loves Starbucks but buys generic coffee and sends the difference to us. Kids donate their birthday money and Christmas gifts. One family in Florida sends us $15 every day. They don't feel comfortable sitting down to dinner unless they've helped Jews. These people ask not to publicize their gifts. They feel that the Lord knows who they are, and seeking publicity would be wrong."

Eckstein himself has no such qualms. In fact, he requires Jewish recipients of evangelical beneficence to publicly acknowledge the source. He has the power, unique among the heads of major Jewish charities (and rare anywhere in the philanthropic world), to write checks at his own discretion, and he wants his donors to see where their money is going. But there is also a strong element of personal vindication in his unceasing efforts for publicity. Gone are the days when the grandees of the Chicago United Jewish Appeal took Eckstein's money on condition that they didn't have to publicly acknowledge its source.

"Jews have such a cynical, negative view of these people," says Eckstein. "There are all sorts of crazy conspiracy theories out there about what the evangelicals want. But they don't have ulterior motives. These are good, religious people who love Israel and want to help. What's the matter with that?"

THE NEXT DAY I met Eckstein at IFJC headquarters, which is situated in a downtown skyscraper overlooking the old Chicago city hall. At ten in the morning, the phones were ringing off the hook. Some callers wanted to make donations. Others just felt like chatting, or asking a question. A young staffer walked among the cubicles with a Jewish prayer shawl in her hand. "There's a man on the phone who bought one of these and he wants to know how to put it on," she said.

"It's called a *tallis*," said another young operator. "Just tell him to put it on with the label on the outside."

At ten-thirty, the staff gathered for its weekly meeting. Thirty people of various religions and races crowded into a conference room. "We're going to need more space soon," sighed Yechiel Eckstein. The Fellowship has moved three times in recent years but what can you do when your gross keeps going up fifteen or twenty percent a year?

Eckstein's staff was expanding, too. The first item on the agenda was to introduce Sandy Rios, the new vice president for strategic initiatives. Rios is a former daytime television talk-show host, and she looks like one. Recently she had been in Washington, D.C., where she served as the president of Concerned Women for America, a conservative family issues group.

The meeting was chaired by George Mamo, Eckstein's second in command. He led the staff through reports on the fellowship's activities and major profit centers. There were individual donors to keep track of and cultivate, tours of Israel to plan, television shoots to schedule, educational material to prepare. One woman related details of a recent fact-finding trip to Siberia. Another described a philanthropy seminar she had attended in Maryland. The tone was entirely businesslike, the only moment of fervor coming when a woman implored her colleagues to keep the communal refrigerator clean.

Finally Eckstein rose to speak. He began with an announcement. The lost tribe of Manasseh (he used the Hebrew pronunciation, *Menashe*) had been discovered in northeastern India. The tribe's authenticity had recently been certified by the Israeli rabbinate, and six thousand of its members wanted to "return" to the Holy Land. Some, as I had already discovered in the grocery store next to Armageddon, were already there. Eckstein intended to bring the others, and had promised the government of Israel the money needed to do it.

I expected this news to electrify the staff of the IFCJ, but it was received instead with an affectionate yawn. That's Rabbi for you, always coming up with something new and different.

TRANSPORTING SIX THOUSAND lost Jews from India to Israel is Indiana Jones stuff, but it is also, inescapably, a political act. Israeli political parties were already tussling over patronage of this potential new voting bloc. Palestinians, meanwhile, were condemning the find as another Jewish trick to upset the demographic balance. They had a point: If rabbis can turn six thousand Indians into biblical Jews and bring them to Israel, what's to stop them from finding six hundred thousand somewhere else?

Eckstein was untroubled by these concerns. Opponents sometimes charge him with being in the pocket of the right-wing settlers, but this is untrue. "I've tried to guide my organization in a nonpartisan way," he says. Eckstein has supported every Israeli government, and hands out money on a transpartisan basis.

In fact, Eckstein's unwillingness to buck the Israeli establishment has put him at odds with some of his more extreme Zionist benefactors, who oppose any Jewish withdrawal from biblical land. A number of right-wing Israeli politicians have made contact with these evangelicals, and some West Bank settlements receive financial aid from them. But the great majority—Eckstein's majority—are content to remain within the boundaries of the prevailing Israeli political consensus.

Eckstein is also somewhat to the left of his constituency on social issues. For most of his life he was a registered Democrat and he endeavors to keep the IFCJ bipartisan in U.S. politics. This is a delicate balancing act, however. Eckstein's Washington lobbying group, Stand For Israel, has been cochaired by Ralph Reed, and this year by former GOP presidential aspirant Gary Bauer. At noon, over tuna sandwiches, Eckstein, Mamo, and Sandy Rios gathered in a small conference room for a telephone with Bauer over the details of an upcoming meeting in Washington.

Eckstein included me in the conversation and invited me to ask questions of Bauer.

"Jews think Christian support for Israel is a trick," I said. "They hear 'evangelical' and think 'anti-Semite.' What do you say to them?"

"There's a lot of history we'd like to do over," Bauer replied. "But this is a new era. Today, Jews are safer living in countries where Christianity is vibrant than they are anyplace else."

Eckstein nodded. "We've got to convince Jews to practice what I call the Four A's," he said. "One, *awareness,* that evangelicals are helping Israel. Two, *acknowledgment* of that help. Three, *appreciation.* And four, *attitude change.* There's been progress on the first two, and number three is coming along, but attitude change remains elusive. I want more than a tactical alliance. I'm looking for genuine fellowship. And the Jewish community is nowhere near that."

"A lot of this is hostility from Jews who just can't stand conservatives," said Bauer. "It trumps even their support for Israel."

"Jews tend to demonize evangelicals," said Eckstein sadly.

"And not the other way around?" I asked.

Eckstein shrugged. "Not really. No."

During this conversation, Sandy Rios had been visibly anxious to join in. After Bauer rang off she cleared her throat and said, "You know, the truth is, Christians *do* want to convert Jews."

Eckstein and Mamo exchanged glances. "Not by some bait-and-switch trick," she added quickly. "We believe it's part of God's plan." Eckstein winced as he had when Pastor Steve introduced

him as a born-again Christian, but Rios didn't notice, or didn't
care. "We love Jews, notwithstanding their rudeness and hatred
for us," she assured me.

Three days later Eckstein called me in New York. Sandy Rios,
he said, had been fired. "It's really my fault," he said. "Hiring staff
is a problem. Truthfully, it's extremely hard to find people who
understand exactly what we're doing here."

NINE

FOXMAN'S COMPLAINT

On November 3, 2005, a year and a day after George W. Bush's reelection, Abraham Foxman, the director of the Anti-Defamation League, declared war on evangelical Christianity.

Speaking at an ADL National Commission meeting, Foxman warned that the Jews faced "a better organized, more sophisticated, coordinated and energized coalition of groups in opposition to our policy positions on church-state separation than ever before. Their goal is to implement their Christian worldview. To Christianize America. To save us!"

Foxman claimed that the forces arrayed against the Jews sought not merely to promote Christian values, but to "actively pursue the restoration of a Christian nation." As exhibit A he offered D. James Kennedy, the Florida televangelist, whom he labeled, with some exaggeration, "one of the most important and influential of today's evangelical leaders."

According to Foxman, the Christian theocrats were just around the bend. "If their agenda was hidden fifteen years ago, today it is in full public view. Just take a look at their websites where they document in considerable detail an agenda on a wide range of issues: judicial nominations, same-sex marriage, and faith-based issues," he said.

Such advocacy amounted, in Foxman's opinion, to "open arrogance." He called on the ADL, and the wider Jewish community, to take immediate action.

No mainstream secular Jewish leader had ever taken such a confrontational line against conservative Christianity. Evidently it didn't occur to Foxman that, as a representative of, at most, less than 2 percent of the population, he himself could be accused of arrogance. It also didn't appear to dawn on him that the very act of taking on millions of evangelicals, including the heads of the party in power, was an act of self-confidence not likely to be undertaken by the spokesman of a genuinely endangered minority.

What Foxman was actually doing, aside from raising money, was turning down the Judeo-Christian bargain the evangelicals had placed on the table.

I first met Abe Foxman in Jerusalem in the late 1970s. He was a rising executive at the Anti-Defamation League, intense, smart, and very ambitious, more hawkish in his foreign policy views than the average American Jewish bureaucrat, Orthodox but not holier-than-thou, a good guy to chat with over a drink. The most interesting thing about him was his biography. He was born in Poland in 1940, saved from the Nazis by a nanny, baptized, and raised as a Catholic until his parents were able to reclaim him a few years later. After he was brought to Brooklyn in 1950, he was raised as a nice Jewish boy. He went to a yeshiva. He graduated from CCNY and NYU Law School. He married a girl named Golda and went to work for the ADL, where he sometimes crossed swords with another young bureaucrat, Yechiel Eckstein. If you had told me when I first knew Foxman that someday he would be a "Jewish leader" bold enough to declare war on Christian America, I would have bet against it.

A few weeks after Foxman's speech, the Reform movement, the country's biggest and most influential Jewish denomination, held its biennial convention in Houston. My boyhood friend Eric Yoffie, now Reform's chief rabbi, took the occasion to denounce the war in Iraq, the Bush administration's domestic policies, and, most sharply, evangelical activists—especially for their opposition to gay marriage, which he likened to Hitler's persecution of homosexuals. I was struck by the aggressive tone of the speech. Yoffie is a very judicious fellow; attacking other religions isn't normally his style.

Soon after, Rabbi James Rudin weighed in with a book titled *The Baptizing of America*. Like Yoffie and Foxman, Rudin is an experienced organization man, a senior official at the very establishment American Jewish Committee. Rudin's book began, "There is a specter haunting America . . . the specter of our nation ruled by the extreme Christian right, who would make the United States a 'Christian Nation' where their version of God's law supersedes all human law—including the Constitution."

Rudin went on to describe visiting friends in Boca Raton, Florida. "My wife and I were stunned to see a skywriter flying just above us spelling out this message: JESUS LOVE US—JESUS IS THE U.S." Rudin took this as a sign that theocratic Christianity was looming just above his head.

Rudin admitted that most evangelical Christians have no intention of turning the United States into a theocracy. The examples he gave of political encroachments were marginal at best. He cited Pat Robertson's unsuccessful run for the Republican presidential nomination in 1988, which he characterized as part of a subversive master plan to replace "the Eagle" with "the Cross." Rudin based this charge primarily on the fact that Robertson had sent his supporters out to Iowa to wage a covert campaign with orders to "give the impression that you are there to work for the party. Hide your strength. Don't flaunt your Christianity."

Rudin portrayed Robertson—and Jerry Falwell, and other political evangelicals—as creatures of two obscure "Christocrat" ideologues, Frances A. Schaeffer and Rousas John Rushdoony. He called Schaeffer the father of dominionism and Rushdoony the propagator of Christian reconstructionism, doctrines, he claimed, that comprise an "ominous belief system that powers much of Christocratic thinking."

In fact, Schaeffer, who wrote mostly in the 1970s and 1980s, never advocated Christian government. Rudin admits as much, but accuses him of encouraging evangelicals to get involved in political life. This is true, but not quite the indictment Rudin regards it as being. "When the United States was founded, the population was pretty close to one hundred percent Christian," Falwell told me. "By 1900 the proportion of Christians declined, and it has been declining ever since. That has been the trend, and it will be the trend fifty years from now. Religion isn't the issue. I'd support Joe Lieberman for a seat on the Supreme Court if he were pro-life. I'd be his campaign manager. It's about principles, not people's religion."

Falwell denied that he and his fellow Baptists are theocrats. "God wants nothing to do with theocracy, I'm sure," he said. "Personally, I'd much rather sit under a political dictator than a religious dictator. Christian government in America would be absolutely ridiculous. Not only do I oppose it, the great majority of American evangelicals oppose it."

As for Rushdoony, who did in fact teach that democracy and biblical law are incompatible, he influenced almost no one and died, in 2001, unknown to almost everyone except conspiracy theorists.

WHILE FOXMAN, YOFFIE, and Rudin were stirring things up on the East Coast, an eccentric lawyer and former Reagan appointee, Mikey Weinstein, was opening a western front in the war against evangelical Christianity at the Air Force Academy in Colorado Springs.

Trouble began when an academy football coach hung an inspirational banner that read, "I am a Christian first and last . . . I am a member of Team Jesus Christ." When people protested that a publicly funded institution couldn't motivate its athletes that way, the banner came down. The academy, sensing trouble, also instituted what it called an RSVP (Respect the Spiritual Values of People) program, but that didn't put an end to the issue. Neither did a meeting between the superintendent of the academy, Lieutenant General John Rosa Jr., and a group of "concerned Jewish civilians." An inspection team from the mainline Yale Divinity School was invited by the academy to look into the situation. They reported "overzealousness" among its evangelical chaplains—not a surprising finding considering the anti-evangelical composition of the investigators. Still, no one had actually uncovered any actual anti-Semitic incidents at the school, much less cases of systemic discrimination or persecution.

Mikey Weinstein was undeterred by this. In October 2005 he filed a federal lawsuit against the air force. He alleged that his sons—one a recent graduate, the other still at the academy—had been subjected to anti-Semitic slurs by evangelical cadets.

The air force reacted to this charge by withdrawing permission from its chaplains to evangelize "unaffiliated" personnel. This incensed Congressman Walter B. Jones of North Carolina, who asked President Bush to issue an executive order guaranteeing First Amendment rights to military chaplains—including the right to pray in their own words. Congressman Steve Israel of Long Island retaliated by calling for a commission to study religious coercion in the military.

The air force, caught in the middle, issued new orders, cautioning superiors not to give their troops any religious messages, overt or subtle. At the same time, it dropped its interim ban on prayer at staff meetings and other officially sanctioned events. The ADL called this a "significant step backwards," while the National Association of Evangelicals (NAE) applauded it.

At this point, the head of the NAE, Reverend Ted Haggard of Colorado Springs, and Mikey Weinstein entered into a fraught correspondence that soon became public. Haggard wrote:

> In some nations, under the banner of freedom of religion, they limit religious speech to anyone but the already converted. To limit freedom of religion, speech, or the press under the guise of freedom of religion, speech, or the press happens often. That's what we're facing with your efforts. But I'm confident authentic freedom will prevail. I think I have a higher view of adults to manage freedom of religion, speech, and the press. I don't believe government supervision is necessary except in extreme cases (Christian or Islamic religious speech used to incite violence, etc.), and that in fact freedom and goodness increase in any society that takes the risk of embracing First Amendment ideas. No doubt, some would rather have government-supervised religion, press, and speech, because it does provide comfort to those who think government supervision of expression is beneficial to their cause, but I think we've proven worldwide that, in most cases, individual freedom is better than increased government regulation.
>
> My concern, though, as I expressed on the phone to you, is not exclusively the American issue, but the global struggle for the advancement of representative government, civil liberties, and fundamental freedom. It is my view that both Christian and Jewish leaders would be wise to unite together

to protect those who are threatened with extermination and death. If Jewish and Christian believers in America remain fractured, we're going to lose too much worldwide. Instead, Christian and Jewish believers need to become friends and work together. . . .

I don't want to get into an e-mail discussion. I just wanted you to know that I'm constantly involved in trying to protect Israel and other international Jewish interests, and find it difficult to defend Jewish causes around the world and, at the same time, have men like yourself trying to use increased government regulation to limit freedom here at home.

This invitation to join Haggard in a Judeo-Christian alliance inspired an outraged retort from Weinstein.

"Men like yourself"?? . . . "your efforts"?? . . . Ted, you have absolutely *no* idea as to what "religious freedom" actually means, apparently!! . . . I'll, too, *not* do this via e-mail, but suffice it to say that I *wholeheartedly* reject en toto your patently ridiculous assertions that me and mine are somehow "hurting" your feelings and trying to restrict *your* religious freedoms . . . your baseless whining and illogical and twisted view of the First Amendment (and utterly warped view of the other relevant and germane parts of our Constitution—see Clause 3 of Article 6!) is not remotely surprising as, without a scintilla of a doubt, you subscribe to the tortured, pedestrian tripe that this wonderful nation's long-standing "tolerance of diversity" is nothing more than evincing "*In*tolerance of the majority" . . . how *dare* you try to assert that me and my supporters are making it *more* difficult for *you* to fight "global anti-Semitism!!!!! . . . ("with friends like you, eh??!!) . . . in other words, you exhibit a boundless hubris in trying to posit that, because we take a firm stand against you and yours, we are, thus, endangering *your* noble national and international efforts to "protect" me, my family, my people and what?? . . . all of the rest of world Jewry too!!?? . . . that unbridled, sanctimoniously triumphant and callous position is nothing less than pitiably shameful, Ted . . . and you *know* it, too!!! . . . shame, Ted, *shame* on you for that!!! . . . please *think* what you just said to me!! . . . that is quite beneath contempt . . . even for you!!! . . . "we" don't depend upon 'ol Ted to be our worldwide protector.

THE FALL OFFENSIVE against evangelical Christianity wasn't coordinated, but it did reflect Jewish public opinion, especially following the reelection of George W Bush. Foxman tried to parlay the mood into a common front by inviting Yoffie and some other Jewish leaders to a summit meeting in late 2005. Only a few turned up, however, and the meeting produced no results. Some who attended thought Foxman had gone too far already. Others simply didn't feel like serving in Abe's army.

A few prominent evangelicals reacted to the attacks from the Jews with anger and threats. Donald Wildmon, leader of the American Family Association and a longtime Christian Zionist, was blunt. "The more he [Foxman] says, 'You people are destroying this country,' you know some people are going to begin to get fed up and say, 'Well, all right then. If that's the way you feel, then we just won't support Israel.'"

This concern was shared by Professor Charles Dunn, dean of the School of Government at Regent University. "We have a tradition in this country," he told me. "We get along."

Dunn is a thoughtful man with a Ph.D. in political science who once served as chief of staff to the New York Republican senator Charles Goodell. "I know there are Jews who fear that we are in favor of a Christian theocracy, but they are just wrong," he said. "Jews mistrust us because they don't understand us. Their mistrust is misplaced. Restorationists are a tiny minority. We evangelicals don't look to the government for our salvation. There are some Jewish leaders, like Abe Foxman, who seem to want enemies. I'm not predicting a backlash, but there could be one. It's possible that in the future some evangelical leaders might say, 'Hey, we've bent over backwards to be friendly with you. We're tired of you always attacking us. Enough is enough.' Only mutual respect will prevent anti-Semitic idiots from ever gaining strength. Abe Foxman isn't in that exact same category, but the animus is there."

Jerry Falwell, on the other hand, was dismissive. "I know Abe Foxman," he told me. "When we meet he acts like I'm his long-lost brother. Then he goes out and attacks evangelicals as a means to raise money. Abe lacks integrity. I have zero respect for him. After his last tirade, Jewish leaders called me and said, 'Don't pay attention to that damn fool.' I don't care how Abe Foxman feels about me, I support Israel because God commands me to."

IN THE SPRING of 2006 Kevin Phillips published *American Theocracy*. Phillips, billed with some exaggeration as "America's premier political analyst," dedicated his book to "the millions of Republicans, present and lapsed, who have opposed the Bush dynasty and the disenlightenment of the 2000 and 2004 elections."

American Theocracy was embraced by the Jewish secular elite. Here was an indictment of rampant evangelical constitutional encroachment written not by a rabbi or Jewish leader but by a former Republican Christian.

But Phillips's warning about theocracy was no more serious

than Rudin's. He defined theocracy as "some degree of rule by religion," a meaningless criterion by which every society this side of Norway is a theocracy. In the real world theocracies are nations ruled by religious leaders (the Cambridge Dictionary definition) who impose their interpretation of holy texts on their fellow citizens, by force if necessary. *Iran* is a theocracy. The United States certainly isn't.

In fact, as Falwell noted, the United States has been moving in the opposite direction for more than two hundred years. The original colonies had state religions. A hundred years ago there were laws against shopping or playing ball on the Christian Sabbath. In my father's lifetime, the government outlawed alcohol for Christian reasons. In mine, abortion and homosexuality were illegal, condoms were kept behind the counter, and you had to go to an Elks Club smoker to see films of women with naked breasts. When I left for Israel in 1967, sit-com couples slept in separate beds and you couldn't say "damn" on the radio. When I came back to visit, less than ten years later, I barely recognized the United States. On my first night I fell asleep with the TV on. In the morning, half-awake, I heard Phil Donahue discussing oral sex with a group of housewives and nearly fell off the couch.

Phillips himself admits that the current level of evangelical political action is a reaction to this almost unbelievable change in public morality and discourse. "When [religion] was trod upon in the 1960s and thereafter by secular advocates determined to push Christianity out of the public square," he wrote, it was "a mistake that unleashed an evangelical, fundamentalist, and Pentecostal counterreformation that in some ways is still building."

Whether militant secularization has been a mistake or not is a matter of opinion. But the charge that the United States is, or is becoming, a theocracy is just silly. It is especially silly for Jews who (correctly) regard Israel as a democracy; the Jewish state comes much closer to being a theocracy than the United States.

Very simply, the United States is too large and too well built to be in any danger from theocrats. The country is protected by its Constitution, its federal system, and its national traditions. The work of separating the religiously conservative from the culturally secular has, for the most part, been done by history, propinquity, and common sense. There is room to accommodate everyone. As Professor Dunn says, people get along. American religious controversies—and certainly the fight between liberal Jews and evangelicals—are mostly theoretical, and to a large extent, contrived, a way to rally voters or raise funds.

Obviously there are real issues. Abortion, gay marriage, prayer in school—these are all serious points of contention. But if *Roe v. Wade* is overturned, abortion will still be legal in the states that want it. Civil unions for gay couples are already available in many places, and gaining. In the era of private schools, vouchers, and de facto segregation in public education, prayer in the classroom is more often than not a matter of local option. In Detroit I once met a high-ranking school official who customarily sent out letters signed, "Yours in Christ." When I pointed out that the Constitution bars that sort of language, the official just laughed and said, "In America, maybe. Not here."

It is also worth remembering that evangelical Christianity, unlike Islam or Judaism, has no book of laws. There is no born-again sharia code or halachic legal system. Restorationists like Rushdoony are forced to fall back on the Old Testament. And my experience with the political rabbis of Jerusalem makes me confident that, as long as Americans love bacon and eggs, Friday-night football, and sexy movies, there's very little chance of an Old Testament regime taking hold in the United States.

• • •

IN EARLY 2006, in the midst of the anti-evangelical campaign, the 92nd Street Y in Manhattan invited Yechiel Eckstein to debate Rabbi David Saperstein, head of Reform Judaism's Religious Action Center in Washington, D.C. Saperstein, who has worked with Eric Yoffie for decades, is a legendary lobbyist with a fine pedigree; his father, Harold Saperstein, was one of the first Amer-ican rabbis to come out against the war in Vietnam. Saperstein has spent his life at the center of left-wing causes, and he is a part of the progressive establishment: a member of the board of the NAACP and People for the American Way and a co-chairman of the Coalition to Preserve Religious Liberty. He's even married to a National Public Radio producer. He is, in short, the very model of a liberal reform activist.

Eckstein started the discussion by making his familiar argu-ment: Christian Zionists, motivated by the biblical covenant be-tween God and the Jews, are reliable friends. There was a scattered applause, but most of the audience was audibly skepti-cal. An elderly couple next to me, wearing his and his earrings, looked at each other and said, simultaneously, "Bullshit." People nearby laughed and nodded.

Saperstein, whose debating style is as peppery as Eckstein's is bland, readily agreed that evangelicals are great supporters of Israel. But he made it clear that this wasn't his priority. He was most concerned by domestic political matters, and he asserted that the evangelicals are motivated by a sense of divine command-ment. "They still believe their covenant is the one true way to heaven," he said. Saperstein wasn't making a competing religious claim; Reform Judaism doesn't really believe in an afterlife. What bothered him was the evangelicals' presumption, as well as their taste in federal judges and their desire to repeal the cultural attitudes of the 1960s.

Saperstein won the audience that night; there's no way that a liberal loses an argument to a conservative at the 92nd Street Y. Saperstein was talking to his own people, New Yorkers whose political consciousness was shaped between Selma and Woodstock. They longed for 1969; they didn't want to believe it was really 1938. But the scoffing wasn't quite so confident as it would have been five years ago, before 9/11. In fact, five years ago, Yechiel Eckstein wouldn't have been invited to the YMHA.

AFTER 9/11, SOME things American Jewish liberals had long ignored became harder to miss. The Arabic translation of *Mein Kampf* was a Middle Eastern bestseller. The Palestinian turndown of a two-state solution at Camp David made it clear that the clash between Israel and the Arabs was not simply a dispute over territory. Islamic heads of state began publicly declaring that the Jews controlled the world in some sort of Zionist plot. Once, the Arab and radical Islamic regimes had contented themselves with denunciations of Israel. Now they were increasingly clear that they regarded not "Israel" but "Jews" as the enemy.

Only a week before Abe Foxman issued his warning against evangelical encroachment, the president of Iran, Mahmoud Ahmadinejad, gave a speech of his own. The occasion was the start of Iran's "World Without Zionism Month."

"God willing," the Iranian president said, "with the force of God behind it, we shall soon experience a world without the United States and Zionism." Ahmadinejad followed up a few days later with a pledge to wipe Israel off the map. Actually, he was simply repeating the official policy of the Islamic republic, a goal

first enunciated by the Ayatollah Khomeini. What made Ahmadinejad's declaration newsworthy was the realization that he was
far along—much further than American intelligence had previously guessed—on the path to acquiring nuclear weapons and the
means to deliver them. Israel was in real danger. And not just
Israel. Ahmadinejad declared that there had been no Holocaust,
that it was all a big Jewish trick designed to steal land that right-
fully belonged to the House of Islam.

The Bush administration took Ahmadinejad seriously and
aimed its diplomacy at hauling Iran into the Security Council—a
necessary diplomatic prelude to sanctions or something stronger.
But Bush went beyond that, with an unprecedented pledge to use
American military might to defend Israel.

Publicly, at least, Israel turned down the offer. Its strategic doctrine has always been that it would defend itself. Privately Israeli
leaders were grateful, and told the president so. But liberal American Jewish activists reacted with discomfort. Word circulated that
Bush's willingness to defend Israel might be a ploy to start another war in the Middle East, or a Rovian gambit to garner Jewish
votes. David Elcott spoke for many when he said, "I don't want
this fight to be between Israel and the Iranians. This has nothing
in particular to do with Israel. The Iranians threaten Turkey and
other countries, too."

The Iranians *do* threaten a lot of other countries, but obliterat-
ing them isn't high on their agenda. Tehran obsesses over two
great enemies, the Big Satan in Washington and the Little Satan
in Jerusalem (they would say Tel Aviv), both of which—in the Iranian view—are controlled by Jews. Jews are the declared enemy of
the Islamic republic, whether David Elcott likes it or not.

And not just of the Islamic republic. Today, it is unmistakable
that Jew-hatred is the lowest common denominator of radical Is-

lamic politics. Like mafia families, Al Qaeda, Hamas, Hezbollah, Islamic Jihad, and the rest are bound together in loose and shifting ties of affinity, different in their ethnicity and ideology, but with a common commitment to jihad. They may fight over turf like the Genoveses and the Bonanos, and squabble over arcane matters of theology—but they share a common enemy—the West in general, the United States and Israel in particular, and especially the "Elders of Zion" who run the world for the benefit of the infidels. Sometimes the links are concrete, in a foot-bone-connected-to-the-ankle-bone sort of way. Hezbollah (which is made up of Shiite Arabs) is the proxy army of Iran (which is a Persian country) in Lebanon and abroad. In 1994, according to American and Israeli intelligence, Hezbollah agents, acting at the behest of the Iranians, blew up the Jewish center in Buenos Aires, killing 85 people and wounding 240.

Hamas is neither Persian nor Shiite. It is a Palestinian Sunni Muslim organization. But it has close ties with Tehran and has trained with Hezbollah in Lebanon. The Hamas Charter, adopted in 1988, states explicitly that the group is a wing of the Muslim Brotherhood, which it calls a "universal" organization. Hamas explicitly rejects any solution to the Palestine problem except holy war and absolute victory over Israel. It considers Jews around the world to be the enemy.

Article 22 of the Hamas Charter accuses Jews of "controlling news agencies, the press, publishing houses, broadcasting stations, and others. With their money they stirred revolutions in various parts of the world with the purpose of achieving their interests and reaping the fruit therein. They were behind the French Revolution, the Communist revolution, and most of the revolutions we heard and hear about, here and there. With their money they formed secret societies, such as Freemasons, Rotary

Clubs, the Lions, and others in different parts of the world for the purpose of sabotaging societies and achieving Zionist interests. With their money they were able to control imperialistic countries and instigate them to colonize many countries in order to enable them to exploit their resources and spread corruption there."

After Hamas's electoral victory in the West Bank and Gaza, in January 2006, its political leader, Khalid Mashal (who lives in exile in Damascus, under the protection of the Ba'athist Syrian government), visited Tehran. There, Ayatollah Ali Khamenei, the supreme spiritual leader of the Islamic Republic of Iran, promised Hamas money and support to defeat the "occupier regime" in Palestine and, presumably, Israel's foreign Jewish enablers.

Al Qaeda, experts correctly point out, is not Persian, Shiite, or Palestinian. It very likely has no direct links to Iran, Hezbollah, or Hamas (although one of its senior leaders, Ayman al-Zawahiri, started out in Egypt's Muslim Brotherhood, the progenitor of Hamas). Al Qaeda is a Sunni Islamist movement whose head, Osama Bin Laden, is a Saudi. But Bin Laden's mentor, a Palestinian cleric named Abdullah Azzam, was also among the creators of Hamas. In 1998, when Bin Laden and four colleagues issued a declaration of war against the West, they called it a "Jihad Against Jews and Crusaders." And, when Al Qaeda attacked the World Trade Center and the Pentagon, they were cheered throughout the Arab world by Sunnis and Shiites alike.

In 2003, Daniel Pearl, a correspondent of the *Wall Street Journal,* was taken captive in Pakistan by an Islamist group. They were not Persians, Saudis, Lebanese, Palestinian, or Egyptian. They were Pakistanis. Their leader, Ahmed Omar Saeed Sheikh, was an émigré, born and raised in Britain. These Islamic radicals cut off Daniel Pearl's head, taped the act, and sent out a videotape titled *The Slaughter of the Spy-Journalist, the Jew Daniel Pearl.*

After 9/11 and the Pearl murder, American Jews began taking security measures. National organizations stepped up contacts with the FBI and local police departments. Individuals canceled business trips and vacations in the Middle East. Synagogues hired armed guards.

Still, people who were thrummingly alive to every theoretical danger from evangelical Christianity tried their best to ignore reality. A majority of the people at the YMHA who came to cheer David Saperstein and boo Yechiel Eckstein were unwilling to be convinced that they were in any real danger. "There's a war going on, in case you haven't noticed," James Rudin wrote in *Baptizing America*. But the "war" he had in mind—the war Rudin and his fellow Jewish liberals wanted—was against Christian fundamentalism and the Republican Party.

THE JEWISH IMPULSE to deny danger, misread political reality, and choose the wrong enemies isn't unique to this generation. The ancient Hebrews were out of Egyptian bondage about ten minutes before they began clamoring to go back. Jews wandered around the world homeless for two thousand years while every other nation got itself a state (even the Belgians figured out nationalism faster). In Eastern Europe, Jews defended themselves by praying to a God who didn't listen or building grandiose political theories about the brotherhood of man that pissed everyone off. When the Zionists came along with a practical plan to create a Jewish state, the vast majority of European Jews preferred life in America—or the ghetto.

The American Jewish establishment was especially obtuse about Hitler. Walter Lippmann, the favorite son of the German-Jewish elite, a man hailed by *Time* as "America's most statesmanly pundit," insisted that Nazi anti-Semitism was trivial, and he simply ignored the Holocaust.

The *New York Times* took a similar see-no-evil approach. Stories about the mass murder of Europe's Jews appeared on its front page only six times in six years. Max Frankel, a refugee who, decades later, became the *Times* editor in chief, has referred to this as "the century's bitterest journalistic failure."

It was also a specifically Jewish failure.

The Sulzberger family, which owned the *Times,* laid down what Frankel calls a guiding principle: "Do not feature the plight of the Jews and take care, when reporting it, to link their suffering to that of many other Europeans." This policy was enforced by the *Times* publisher, Arthur Hays Sulzberger, who was a trustee of Temple Emanu-El, New York's cathedral of high Reform Judaism. According to Frankel, Sulzberger thought that "Jews should be separate only in the way they worshipped . . . they needed no state or political or social institutions of their own."

The *Times'* act of journalistic denial was especially odd because so many of its readers had blood relatives who were among Hitler's victims. The paper took a pass on what was essentially a hometown story while customers, many removed from the killing fields of Europe by only a decade or two, said nothing.

Jewish organizations were hardly better. Some were intimidated by isolationists like Charles Lindbergh who accused them of trying to drag the United States into war for their own interests. Others were simply unable to grasp what was happening. And some were less innocent. When Germany signed a nonaggression pact with the USSR, some Jewish communists in the United States were prepared to live with the Nazis—a willingness that ended only after Hitler broke the pact and invaded the USSR.

For the liberal majority, Jewish solidarity simply came in a distant second to political loyalty to Franklin Delano Roosevelt. There were no mass protests in 1939 when FDR refused to let an ocean liner, the *St. Louis,* carrying nine hundred Jewish refugees from Germany, dock in the United States. After Pearl Harbor, mainstream Jewish leaders failed to press the U.S. government to take special measures to save the Jews of Europe. When Rabbi Stephen Wise dared broach the subject, FDR brushed him off with the grand observation that "the mills of history grind slowly."

Ironically, a lot of evangelicals were more clear-sighted. Some saw Hitler as the agent of God's prophesied punishment of the Jews for their sins (there were Orthodox rabbis who preached their own version of this divine-wrath theory), but others tried to mobilize public opinion. In 1939, the *Moody Monthly,* one of the most influential evangelical publications in the United States, ran an article titled "An Appeal for Persecuted Israel," which presciently reported that the lives of 6 million European Jews were in jeopardy. Many evangelical leaders were able to understand that Hitler's anti-Semitism was not some personal quirk but an essential element of his program.

Yechiel Eckstein spoke at the 92nd Street Y as an advocate for the grandsons of these Christian Zionists. He believed, as they did, that Jews were once more threatened by armed, mobilized enemies around the world, and that these threats should be taken personally by the Jews of America. Saperstein, Rudin, Foxman, and the others might be worried about gay marriage or prayer in school—certainly these were valid concerns—but they were not, in a time of jihad, the Jewish existential and moral priority. There was indeed a war going on—and the evangelical Christians, like them or not, were on our side.

The old guys with the earrings sitting next to me at the Y that night mumbled "Bullshit"; it was a message they weren't able to hear. But others—at the YMHA and around the country—were listening, and at least some were thinking a new thought: maybe Eckstein was right; maybe the war against the evangelicals was the wrong war.

TEN

IRAQ: "IT'S NOT MY PROBLEM"

A majority of Jews, like a majority of all Americans, initially supported the decision to invade Iraq. They believed, as almost everyone did, that Saddam Hussein had weapons of mass destruction. They also know, as many Americans did not, that Saddam had fired Scuds at Israel in the first Gulf War. But even Jews who had no special concern for Israel were alarmed by the mushroom clouds the Bush administration invoked.

Most also shared the wider belief that Saddam Hussein and Osama Bin Laden were connected. And, of course, there *was* a connection. The 9/11 Commission found no operational link; Saddam wasn't involved in the plot to attack the World Trade Towers. But the commission noted contact between them. Bin Laden had "explored possible cooperation" with Iraq when Al Qaeda was still based in the Sudan, in the mid-1990s. And terrorist leader Abu Musab al-Zarqawi had indeed been in Iraq before the American invasion, getting treatment in a Baghdad hospital. No foreigners—certainly no battle-hardened foreign fighters with Al Qaeda connections, like al-Zarqawi—were allowed to come to the Iraqi capital without government permission. No hospital would have dared to admit anyone like al-Zarqawi without an okay from Saddam.

In any event, the strategic relationship between 9/11 and Iraq did not depend on a specific operational connection between Al Qaeda and Saddam (or Hezbollah, about which the commission also speculated). For Middle Eastern groups and governments hostile to the United States (as Saddam certainly was), seeing the Twin Towers fall and the Pentagon on fire excited new thoughts about American vulnerability.

The invasion of Iraq was an assault on that excitement, an attempt to reestablish American deterrence. Iraq was chosen not because it was in league with Bin Laden, but because it is at the heart of the Arab world, and because Saddam, the man who stood up the United States in 1991 and lived to tell the story, was an idol of anti-American Arab radicals. By toppling him, the United States was sending a message: if we even *think* you'd do something like 9/11, you're gone.

This was immediately grasped by the dictators of the Arab world. Muammar Qaddafi turned Libya's nuclear program over to the Americans. Mubarak of Egypt and King Abdullah of Jordan tightened already close relations with Washington. The Gulf States allowed themselves to become virtual American military installations. North African regimes even conducted joint naval operations with the American fleet.

What Bush did in Iraq was not the product of crusader zeal or a naïve Wilsonian desire to democratize the region. It was a calculated punch to the Arab solar plexus. On 9/11, Arabs had attacked the United States, and everyone in the Middle East was waiting to see what the Americans would do about it. If Bush had contented himself with an action in Afghanistan, which is far from the Arab world, it would have been interpreted as an evasion and a sign of weakness, like Reagan idly bombing the Syrian countryside from the sea after pulling U.S. Marines out of Beirut in 1983, or Clinton lobbing cruise missiles at the empty tents of Al Qaeda in Afghanistan.

The problem was, Bush couldn't go to the country with this sort of Middle Eastern realpolitik. Americans want to be John Wayne, not Don Corleone. And so the president based his case on a simple and frightening scenario—Iraq had weapons of mass destruction it might pass off to terrorists—that the public could easily grasp.

This was not entirely cynical on Bush's part. The CIA and the Defense Department told him that Saddam had such weapons. It would have been a foolhardy president who brushed off such assessments by his own intelligence services on such a potentially life-threatening issue. But Bush was very probably set on going to Iraq very soon after 9/11 because he wanted to deliver a message, weapons of mass destruction or not.

When it became clear that there were no nuclear or biological weapons in Iraq, and only a few outdated chemical missiles, alternative explanations for the war sprang up. Some said that Bush had been trying to impress his father. Others claimed that he went to war for Halliburton, or big oil, or to win elections. A few, like Senator Fritz Hollings of South Carolina and Representative James Moran of Virginia, charged that Bush had launched the war on behalf of Israel. This idea, widely believed by European elites and taken as a matter of course in the Arab world, permeated parts of the American academic left, nativist right, and "realist" foreign policy circles in Washington.

In the spring of 2006, the thesis that the Jews were behind the war in Iraq found its first full American expression in a paper published by Stephen Walt, the academic dean of Harvard's Kennedy School, and Professor John Mearsheimer of the University of Chicago.

The professors described a Jewish cabal that extended beyond the Bush administration. They pointed out that during the Clinton years three senior State Department officers, Dennis Ross, Martin Indyk, and Aaron Miller (all Jews), had colluded to shape U.S. government policy on Israel's behalf. "Palestinian negotiators complained that they were 'negotiating with two Israeli teams—one displaying an Israeli flag, and one an American flag,'" Walt and Mearsheimer noted.

The professors found the alleged cabal "even more pronounced in the Bush administration, whose ranks have included such fervent advocates of the Israeli cause as Elliot Abrams, John Bolton, Douglas Feith, I. Lewis ("Scooter") Libby, Richard Perle, Paul Wolfowitz, and David Wurmser. As we shall see, these officials have consistently pushed for policies favored by Israel and backed by organizations in the [Zionist] Lobby." All the Bush officials named by Walt and Mearsheimer are Jews except for John Bolton; perhaps they confused him with Josh Bolten, another senior Bush aide who is Jewish.

Walt and Mearsheimer widened the conspiracy to include not only aforementioned officials but Professor Bernard Lewis, journalists William Kristol, Robert Kagen, and Charles Krauthammer. At one point, they even included the *New York Times* in their Jewish lobby. They contended that the nefarious conspiracy has also subverted the nation's think tanks, attempted to silence dissent through blacklists and boycotts, intimidated both political parties and Congress, and generally forced the United States to act against its own interests.

The paper caused a stir. The Kennedy School published what amounted to a disclaimer (proving, in Walt-Mearsheimer World, that Zionist neocons are far along in their plan to take over Harvard and the rest of academia). When pro-Israeli groups complained about the conspiracy theory, Walt and Mearsheimer countered that Zionists always answer their critics by calling them anti-Semites. The accusation that the Jews were behind the war grew so pervasive that at one point, President Bush was moved to publicly deny it.

A delicious response to all this came from David Duke, the former Grand Wizard of the Ku Klux Klan. "I have read one summary [of the Walt-Mearsheimer paper] already and I am surprised how excellent it is," he was quoted as saying by the *New York Sun.* "It is quite satisfying to see a body in the premier American university essentially come out and validate every major point I have been making even before the war started. . . . The task before us is to wrest control of America's foreign policy and critical junctures of media from the Jewish extremist neo-cons." Duke's endorsement was echoed by the head of the Guidance Council of the Egyptian Muslim Brotherhood, Abd al-Mun'im Abu al-Futuh, who observed that "the people who wrote the report were working in the interest of the American people."

Even before the Walt-Mearsheimer paper, I had discussed the accusation of neocon perfidy with one of the supposed members of the cabal, Jay Lefkowitz. He is a thin, redheaded man with a slight lisp who doesn't look old enough to vote, let alone serve in high-ranking White House positions. But he was a senior aide in the first Bush II administration and, because he is Orthodox, something of an adviser on Jewish matters. Once, before a state dinner, Laura Bush called him to ask about the rules for mixing meat and dairy. He told her that it was forbidden.

"If we have fish instead of meat, will everyone be able to eat?" she asked.

"Well, no," he admitted. He suggested giving the Orthodox guests separate dishes and silverware, but Mrs. Bush wasn't willing to do that. She ordered kosher dishes and silverware for everyone. "It was the first time in American history they didn't use the official china at a state dinner," said Lefkowitz.

Lefkowitz didn't deal with the Middle East during his years at the White House. But he is outraged by the suggestion that Jews who did had hoodwinked the United States into going to war. "There weren't any Jews in Bush's war cabinet," he told me. "Who were the Jews? Dick Cheney? Condi Rice? Colin Powell? George Tenant? Donald Rumsfeld? Those were the people who made the decisions, not their deputies and assistants."

I WAS ESPECIALLY pleased by the fact that Walt and Mearsheimer named me as one of the co-conspirators. In fact, I have never met Bill Kristol, Elliot Abrams, Paul Wolfowitz, Richard Perle, Douglas Feith, Scooter Libby, or any of the other Elders of Zion. I did, however, write a number of columns in the New York *Daily News* advocating American action to depose Saddam and his regime. I wrote as an Israeli (albeit one with American citizenship) and out of personal experience. Saddam Hussein had tried to kill my son and me.

In 1990, in the approach to the first Gulf War, as American and coalition forces assembled in Saudi Arabia, Saddam announced that he would retaliate for any attack by "burning half of Israel." I was working for the *Jerusalem Report* at the time, and we tried desperately to find out what Iraqi assets lay behind that threat. Some Mossad analysts thought Saddam had at least one dirty bomb that could be used to contaminate Tel Aviv. Others believed he had chemical weapons. A few thought he might even have a nuke bought on the black market. Nobody was certain.

The government decided to pass out gas masks to the entire population and required people to prepare a "safe room" at home. There was a run on bottled water, masking tape, sheets of transparent plastic (to seal windows), transistor radios, and anything else people believed might come in handy during a nuclear, chemical, or biological attack.

Saddam struck on the first night of the war. We were awakened in Tel Aviv at two in the morning by air-raid sirens, and by the time we had put on our masks and sealed ourselves in our safe room (which was also the bathroom), the first Scud missiles had already fallen, one not far from my house. We felt the impact, heard the sirens, and tightened the straps on our masks. A government spokesman on the radio warned everyone to stay put until it could be determined if the missiles had released poisons.

They hadn't, but I didn't want to take chances on the future. I called a friend of mine, a senior Israeli official with a lifetime of experience in security matters and access to the country's most sensitive information. "I've got to ask you one question," I said. "I know you can't tell me details, but if you were me, and you had an eight-year-old son, would you bring him to Jerusalem or let him stay in Tel Aviv?" Speculation was that the Iraqis wouldn't dare fire missiles at Jerusalem and risk hitting the Dome of the Rock and the Mosque of Omar, among Islam's holiest shrines.

My friend, a Holocaust survivor, prided himself on his unflappable stoicism. Once, when we were both in Egypt on Israeli government business, we had been stalked for a week by a Palestinian hit team. When the terrorists were caught, and the plan exposed, I learned that my friend had known about it the whole time. He hadn't said anything, and I hadn't sensed a problem. When I had mentioned this to him later, he had shrugged and said, "What happens, happens. You didn't need to know." That was the kind of dismissive macho attitude I wanted to hear from him now. But without hesitation he said, "I'd bring my son to Jerusalem."

A lot of people came to the same conclusion; Tel Aviv and other coastal cities emptied out. School was called off, men and

women didn't go to work or leave the house at night. Movies, con-
certs, and shows were canceled, restaurants and bars closed. The
national radio broadcast a silent channel—you could leave it on
while you slept and it would only activate for alerts. The Iraqis
fired thirty-nine salvos at Israel over the course of the Gulf War.
Every time I had to look into my son's eyes as I fitted him with his
gas mask.

Seven years later, Saddam Hussein kicked UN weapons inspec-
tors out of Iraq, and the United States threatened action. We
feared that Israel would once again be Saddam's default target.
Chief UN inspector Richard Butler told interviewers that Saddam
had biological weapons sufficient to wipe out Tel Aviv. The Israeli
government instructed the public not to panic—and announced
that it would be passing out updated gas masks.

By now my son Shmulik was fifteen, old enough to put on his
own mask. But Lisa and I had little kids, a two-year-old son and a
baby daughter. They were too small for gas masks. We went to the
Yad Eliahu basketball stadium, suddenly transformed into a civil
defense center, and picked up tiny protective tents for the kids.
Then we went home and waited to see if Richard Butler was
right.

So, when the United States went to war in Iraq in 2003, did I
believe that Saddam Hussein might very well have weapons of
mass destruction? Did I think he would fire them at Tel Aviv? Did
I want him—for Israeli reasons, Jewish reasons, personal reasons—
gone? Damn right I did. Saddam was far more than a Jewish or
Israeli problem—if he had been only that, George H. W. Bush
would never have gone after him in the first Gulf War—but, like
so many enemies of civilization, past and current, he had a special
thing about Jews, Israel, and Zionists. He gave stipends to Palestinians who killed Israelis. He talked openly of torching Israel.
George H. W. Bush exaggerated in the first Gulf War when he

compared Saddam to Hitler, but Saddam had a Nazi attitude toward the Jewish state. Getting rid of him was, in my opinion, good for the United States *and* for Israel.

THIS OPINION WAS not universally shared by the Jewish community. By the 2004 presidential election, Iraq had become a partisan issue—and most Jews are Democrats. In November, at the Reform movement's biennial convention in Houston, Eric Yoffie used the occasion not only to castigate the evangelical right but to attack the war. He steered through a resolution excoriating Bush's "failures before and during the war" and called for a "clear exit strategy with specific goals for troop withdrawal." These demands were couched in biblical and Talmudic citations on the subject of "just war," but the stance was political, not theological; the resolution itself made that clear.

"American opinion, and Jewish opinion in particular, has turned against the war," it said. "Nearly two-thirds of Americans disapprove of the Administration's handling of the situation in Iraq and would favor removing some or all troops from Iraq. Moreover, Americans are uneasy about the rising price tag for the war, which has already cost over $200 billion, diverting money and resources that are urgently needed at home. Some have argued that future generations will continue to have to pay this cost, as a result of concurrent tax cuts coupled with spending of borrowed funds. Two-thirds of American Jews now describe the war as a mistake and a majority seeks to bring American troops safely and speedily home."

Passing this resolution made Yoffie's movement the first mainstream Jewish group to join the antiwar coalition. But this created a problem. The antiwar coalition was led by stridently anti-Israeli factions.

"Sadly," the resolution noted, "within the organized opposition to the war there are a number of groups espousing radical, anti-Israel rhetoric (including a number of members of ANSWER—Act Now to Stop War and End Racism). In a second major coalition, United for Peace and Justice, there are fewer such voices. But the absence of mainstream American Jewish organizations from this debate has created a vacuum in which other voices are manipulating messages about Jews and Israel in the context of and in opposition to the Iraq war."

This Houston convention marked a return to the 1960s, when the Reform movement had been an integral part of the antiwar camp. But this time it was an uncomfortable fit. Back then, we were thrilled when Muhammad Ali refused induction into the army on the grounds that "no Vietnamese ever called me nigger." It wasn't his fight, and it wasn't ours, either. But the war in Iraq was a different matter. Like it or not, Saddam Hussein had not only called Jews "nigger," but fired weapons at them. The forces battling in Iraq after Saddam's fall—Sunni Ba'athists, Arab nationalists, Al Qaeda terrorists, Shiite Iranian surrogates—were all bitter enemies of Israel and the Jews. The future governance of Iraq, the military posture of the United States in the Middle East, the broader war on Islamic terrorism—all these were inescapably Jewish issues whether Jews wanted them to be or not.

Jewish denial of the obvious implications of Iraq, and the broader jihad, was reflected in the fact that few young American Jews joined the U.S. military. The community dealt with the armed forces as alien territory, of interest primarily for their discriminatory policies toward gays and women, their role in the military-industrial complex, or, in the case of the Air Force Academy, as a supposed hotbed of right-wing evangelicalism.

Rabbi Carlos Huerta is the Jewish chaplain of West Point. I met him not long after the Reform movement passed its anti-Iraq resolution at the military academy's Jewish Chapel, a small, modern building whose walls are decorated with laminated baseball cards of Jewish major-leaguers, military scenes from the Old Testament, and plaques bearing the names of 16 Jewish Congressional Medal of Honor winners and the 821 Jewish graduates of West Point since Simon Levy, class of 1802.

Huerta is a giant, six feet five at least and close to 300 pounds, with an open, friendly face that looks more Aztec than Ashkenazi. He was just back from a tour of duty in Iraq and expected to be going again soon, and he was still wearing combat fatigues.

"I have kids who come here, they don't want the people at their synagogue to know they're going to West Point," he said. "Jewish kids in America know everything, but if you ask them to name some Jewish Medal of Honor winners, they don't know what you're talking about. Ask them about General Shaknow [a concentration camp survivor who came to the United States and became the commander of the Special Forces] and they look at you blankly. 'General Shaknow? Never heard of him.'"

Huerta knows there are charges that the Jews aren't doing their share in the fight against Islamic radicals. "I've heard people say, 'Jews consume freedom, they don't manufacture it,'" he said. "That kind of talk hurts morale. We just buried a young Jewish woman MP in Iraq. There were plenty of Jews over there. I was in a Special Forces compound not long ago, near Mosul, where some guys came over to me and said, 'Hey, Rabbi, can you get us siddurs [prayer books]?' Plenty of Jews."

Plenty is a relative term. The army doesn't publish statistics, but the usual estimate is that Jews make up less than 2 percent of the military, and many are recent immigrants from the former USSR or Israel.

There are about seventy Jews at West Point. They have a choir, a Hillel, and a newspaper, *The Tablets,* whose masthead bears the words of George Orwell: "We sleep at night because rough men stand ready to visit violence on those who would harm us."

That weekend, the Jewish cadets were scheduled to host the Jewish students of the Naval Academy and the Air Force Academy for a long Shabbat. One of the planners was Britney Berkoff, a tall, blond cadet, daughter of a Jewish Special Forces officer who graduated from West Point in 1981 and a Hispanic mother who converted to Judaism.

"I got into the Academy as a Hispanic minority admission," Berkoff told me, "but during Beast Barracks I noticed that the Jewish upperclassmen didn't haze us. They were actually *nice* to us. They even let us use their phones. So I decided to join the Jewish Club."

Berkoff has discovered that, beyond the walls of the academy, the Jewish club isn't so easily approached. "We went to Vassar for a Shabbat at the Hillel not too long ago and it was very uncomfortable," she recalled. "Everyone was so against the war. They said, 'The *army?* Why do *that?*' I mean, they were nice and welcoming in a way. We had services together. But it was like they were almost attacking us. We said, 'We want to serve our country,' which they didn't seem to understand exactly. But for me, it's pretty simple. I plan to lead troops into battle and bring them back alive."

Donald Benjamin, class of '08, wouldn't be attending the Shabbat weekend. A sturdy-looking young man with a baby face and an excitable disposition, he was due to spend the weekend at home, in Phoenix. He was sorry to miss the occasion, because he saw himself as a role model. "Most of the Jews here are only half-Jewish," he said. "I'm a full-blooded Jew, on both sides. My goal here is to shatter every Jewish stereotype. If I go someplace and you're supposed to bring flowers, I buy twice as many as anyone else. I don't want people to think I'm cheap. I went to high school in Phoenix with about seven Jewish kids, and they upset me with how stereotypical they acted."

"Stereotypical how?"

Benjamin glanced at my notebook and paused. "Chicken shit," he said.

He had been in Israel the previous summer and fell for the macho spirit of the place. "Israelis are a different breed of Jew," he said approvingly. He told me he keeps an Israeli flag folded up in his barracks room. "I'm super pro Israeli."

Benjamin feels—as most American Jews his age evidently do not—that the jihad, including the war in Iraq, is his fight. "[The kind of anti-Semitism in the Middle East] enrages me," he said. "I *do* take it personally. Here, the way we live, everything seems to be happening worlds away. You grow up in a rich neighborhood and you learn to look out for yourself. I hate to say it, but most American Jews look at what's happening in the world and they say, 'It's not my problem.'"

ELEVEN

JEWS ARE DEMOCRATS, ISRAELIS ARE REPUBLICANS

In May 2004, President George W. Bush had the strange experience of giving a speech to a mostly Democratic Jewish audience that loved him. He was interrupted twenty times with wild applause, and won himself a standing ovation. "The Israeli people have always had enemies at their borders and terrorists close at hand," he told the national convention of the American-Israel Public Affairs Committee (AIPAC). "Again and again, Israel has defended itself with skill and heroism, and as a result of the courage of the Israeli people, Israel has earned the respect of the American people."

Bush tied Israel to his policies in the Middle East:

On September 11, 2001, Americans saw that we are no longer protected by geography from the dangers of the world. We experienced the horror of being attacked in our homeland, on our streets, and in places of work. And from that experience came an even stronger determination, a fierce determination to defeat terrorism and to eliminate the threat it poses to free people everywhere.

Not all terrorist networks answer to the same orders and same leaders, but all terrorists burn with the same hatred. They hate all who reject their grim vision of tyranny. They hate people who love freedom. They kill without mercy. They kill without shame. And they count their victories in the death of the innocent. . . .

Freedom-loving people did not seek this conflict. It has come to us by the choices of violent men, hateful men. See, we seek peace. We long for peace. Israel longs for peace. America longs for peace. Yet, there can be no peace without defending our security. There is only one path to peace and safety. America will use every resource we have to fight and defeat these enemies of freedom.

Bush's reception at AIPAC was a source of great expectations for Republican strategists. Some predicted that the president would get 35 or even 40 percent of the Jewish vote in 2004. Bush had the tacit endorsement of Prime Minister Ariel Sharon. He was the man who toppled Saddam Hussein (which, in early 2004, was still regarded as politically positive). He was the commander in chief of forces fighting Bin Laden and his "jihad against Jews and crusaders." He had vowed, in strong, clear language, not to allow the genocidal Iranian regime get its hands on nuclear weapons. All of this got George W. Bush 24 percent of the Jewish vote. American Jews might be grateful, and they might be Zionists, but they were, first of all, Democrats.

BACK IN THE days of Abe Lincoln and Teddy Roosevelt, American Jews (at least in the North) were mostly Republicans. But then came the huge influx of Eastern European immigrants, many of whom, like my father's father, were socialists. In the 1920 presidential election, a plurality voted for Socialist Party candidate Eugene V. Debs, who was so revered that the Yiddish-speaking Workmen's Circle, which owned a radio station in New York, gave it the call letters WEVD, the candidate's initials.

FDR turned these Jews into Democrats, and the conversion has, with a few wobbles, stuck. As Richard Brookhiser once observed, the only difference between the Democratic Party and Reform Judaism is the holidays. In a 2005 survey, 54 percent of Jews identified as Democrats, 16 percent as Republicans. According to a study conducted at Denison College in 2000, about 95 percent of Reform, Conservative, and Reconstructionist clergy (and 75 percent of the Orthodox) called themselves Democrats.

These are statistics that the man I'll call The Professional knows by heart. He is a Democratic operative, a pro who has mastered every nuance of Jewish politics in the United States, starting, as politics often do, with the Democratic Party's finances.

"You can replace Jewish votes, which might be four percent nationally," he told me one day over lunch in Washington. "But you can't replace Jewish money. Big-donor lists begin at twenty-five thousand dollars, and at that level of national politics, forty to fifty percent are Jews. The higher the bracket goes up, the higher the percentage."

The *Washington Post* once estimated that Jews contribute 60 percent of the Democratic Party's money. This made The Professional laugh. "We have an internal survey that puts it closer to eighty percent," he said. "We don't publicize it, but Jews contribute more to the party than any other ethnic group. Hell, we contribute more than everybody else put together."

This is not quite the Zionist cabal that Mearsheimer, Walt, and their fellow conspiracy theorists believe. For one thing, Jews—even Democratic Jews—are far from monolithic in their support for Israel. In 2004, when so-called 527 Organizations were the

chief conduit for serious political money, the top four contributors were George Soros, Peter Lewis, Steven Bing, and the Sandler
family. They gave pro-Kerry groups a combined $73 million. This
figure was roughly as much as the next twenty contributors, Republican and Democrat, *combined*. But Soros is no Zionist; in fact,
he believes that Israeli policies are a cause of anti-Semitism. This
is an extreme view among Jewish liberals, but it is by no means
unique. Israel's main supporters in the United States may be Jews,
but so are many of its most prominent critics.

A well-known political cliché holds that American Jews earn
like Episcopalians and vote like Puerto Ricans. This is meant to
convey the idea that Jews are so liberal and altruistic that they
vote against their own interests. But voting Democratic *is* a Jewish
interest. Jews are major stakeholders in the party, which tends to
reflect both their economic concerns and their cultural and ideological sensitivities. Internationalists like Soros and show business
figures whose foreign income is dependent upon American popu-
larity abroad tend to take a "European" view of the Arab-Israel
conflict. Less exalted, grassroots Jews often belong to "helping"
professions, the trial bar, or academics—all areas with a direct interest in big government.

Republicans sometimes talk about the critical influence of Jews
in the Democratic Party in code—"liberal elites," "the Upper West
Side," or "Hollywood." These are euphemisms, of course, but not
necessarily bigoted. On the contrary, they are a polite way of describing a reality that causes uneasiness among some Jewish Democrats.

"You and I can tell who's Jewish and who isn't," The Professional told me. "Most Americans can't."

Actually, most Americans probably can. It doesn't take much
ethnic acuity to notice that Jews comprised 20 percent of the

Democratic senatorial delegation in the 109th Congress or that both Democratic Supreme Court justices, Ruth Bader-Ginsberg and Stephen Breyer, are Jews, or that a very high percentage of the Democratic policy intelligentsia—at magazines like the *New Republic, The Nation,* and *American Prospect,* and think tanks such as the Saban Institute (named for Haim Saban, an Israeli-American and one of the party's chief West Coast moneymen)—are Jewish.

During the Clinton administration, there were five Jewish cabinet officers. The national security adviser was Sandy Berger. The best-known diplomat was Richard Holbrooke. Even Clinton's "goyim"—Secretary of Defense William Cohen (who walked away from the tribe after a rabbi refused to allow him to become bar mitzvah because his mother wasn't Jewish) and Secretary of State Madeline Albright (who had a reporter-assisted recovered memory of her family's ethnicity) were Jewish.

"Jews contribute more than money to the party," said The Professional. "We're a necessary piece of the progressive movement. We are its leaders, in fact. The Ivy League is one-third Jewish these days. MoveOn is funded by Jews. All the major advocacy groups—People for the American Way, the ACLU, the Human Rights organizations, NOW, even some of the labor unions—rely on Jewish leadership. Take the Jews away from the progressive movement and what's left?

"As far as Israel is concerned, let's be realistic. Half the Jews in the nation aren't going to vote against a Democrat no matter what. If Howard Dean had run as the candidate in 2004, he would have gotten sixty-five percent. Nominate Jimmy Carter and he'd get sixty percent. Cynthia McKinney? That one would break fifty-fifty."

The Professional doesn't believe that many Jews will go for the Judeo-Christian bargain offered by Republican evangelicals. "The only place Democrats are vulnerable to this is among Orthodox Jews and among men over thirty-five, because of the war on terror," he said. "In general, it's very hard to get Jews to vote for people who believe that the world was created five thousand years ago. And as far as Jewish women are concerned, Democrats always get eighty to ninety percent. On choice, even Orthodox women are off the charts on the liberal side."

AMONG THE DEMOCRATIC stalwarts I talked to, none was more stalwart than Shira Dicker. Dark-eyed and intense, she works out daily at the Jewish center on Amsterdam Avenue on Manhattan's Upper West Side and holds business meetings at the Starbucks around the corner. Dicker is a public relations consultant who works mostly for liberal Jewish organizations. But on the evening we met for coffee, in late November 2005, she was still recovering from a close encounter with the Christian right.

I was first introduced to Dicker a few months earlier at the Marriott Hotel in Washington, D.C., where she was handling publicity for Yechiel Eckstein's annual Stand For Israel conference, a two-day affair put together by Eckstein's consultant, Gary Bauer, and attended by a mixed bag of Israel lovers. These included multi-millionaires from Toronto and Chicago, a guy from California staying at a D.C. mansion where residents pray four hours a day for Israel in lieu of rent, a contingent of students from Oral Roberts University, a Kansas housewife who runs a pro-Israel lobby from her back porch, a Brooklyn-based Jamaican Pentecostal Zionist, a smattering of Orthodox rabbis, and hundreds of rank-and-file evangelicals. None of these were Shira Dicker's people.

Or Calev Ben-David's. A consultant for a Washington-based Jewish advocacy outfit called "The Israel Project," Ben-David opened the conference with a sophisticated PowerPoint presentation on how to counter Arab arguments and influence the mainstream media. But the presentation left the audience cold. The people at the Marriott supported Israel because the Bible told them to; they didn't understand why they needed additional ammunition.

Rabbi Eckstein rose and saved the moment. "This battle is really a *spiritual* battle," he said. "We are all here because we believe in God's promise to Israel. That's what we want our friends in the Jewish leadership to understand." The crowd applauded loudly. This was the kind of talk they wanted to hear.

Stand For Israel was a hot ticket for ambitious pols. Senators Rick Santorum and Sam Brownback and Republican Representative Mike Pence addressed the plenum. They were Republicans, and so was a large majority of the conferees. Eckstein tries for bipartisanship; in 2003, Stand For Israel honored Democrat Tom Lantos and Republican Tom DeLay. This year, Rudy Giuliani and Joe Lieberman were slated. DeLay was scheduled to give the keynote address, but on the morning of the banquet, word came from Texas that he had been indicted for allegedly laundering campaign money. Everyone expected he would cancel.

Shira Dicker learned at three in the afternoon that DeLay was planning to keep the date. "I was torn," she says. "Personally, I thought, 'This scumbag is our speaker tonight?' But from a professional point of view, I was getting all these calls from the national media. I didn't know if it was great or horrible."

The audience in the packed hotel ballroom that evening had no such uncertainty. DeLay entered to a standing ovation and gave a stem-winding Zionist speech. His appearance made national headlines. It was a triumph of the 'just-spell-my-name-right' school of public relations. And it made Dicker decide to quit.

The International Fellowship of Christians and Jews beat her to the punch; her contract was terminated right after the event.

Dicker wasn't sure why, but she took it as a positive development.

"I just don't feel comfortable with Republicans," she told me. "I think this is the worst administration in American history. I'm contemptuous of them. George W. Bush is a joke. I think *he* thinks he's a joke."

Dicker is the daughter of a liberal rabbi. Her husband, Ari Goldman, was a religion writer for the *New York Times* before becoming a professor of journalism at Columbia University. Stand For Israel offended her because she perceived it as an attack on the separation of church and state and, almost as inexcusable, on the *New York Times*.

"The White House briefing [of Stand For Israel] made me sick," she said. "I mean, Elliot Abrams blamed the *Times* for misquoting Condi Rice."

"The *Times* did misquote her."

"Yeah, well . . . but all those people just cheered Abrams on. And they said *a prayer*. I just don't think that's appropriate to be praying in the White House. These people want to Christianize America."

"The prayer was delivered by a rabbi," I pointed out.

"Okay. Maybe. But I still wasn't comfortable. These people have a grand plan. The Iraq war fits in with a larger scheme. I don't know how. But I do know I'm not comfortable in America today."

Dicker was also upset by the terminology she heard at the conference. "Gary Bauer kept saying, 'Islamo-fascism.' He doesn't say, 'Let's reach out to moderate Muslims.' He should say that, even if we know in our heart that it's useless. We have to at least pay lip service to the idea of reaching out to Islam. Don't misunderstand. I think Gary Bauer is okay. But did you see G. Gordon Liddy at the dinner? *G. Gordon Liddy?* I mean, I don't want him at *my* bar mitzvah."

Dicker isn't what she would call prejudiced. In fact, she pointed out, her nanny is a born-again Christian, albeit a liberal one. But this was different.

"These Christian evangelicals love Jews in an almost get-on-my-nerves way. I sat with this couple at the banquet that was just so *pleased* to be dining with a member of the Chosen People. They were sweet, a lot of the evangelicals are, but their leaders? Ugh."

Dicker was once an executive at the left-leaning New Israel Fund. "For a long time I bought Yechiel Eckstein's line that Jews should cooperate with evangelicals when possible. It's like having friends with terrible taste in music—just don't go to the concert with them. But I've come to see that their leaders are corrupt, horrible people. People in cahoots with Bush. If we cede power to right-wing Christians, we'll be marginalized. We'll have a Christian America. I'm glad they support Israel, but I just no longer felt I could put my name on the press releases. To me it's a moral issue."

Moral or political? Dicker considered. "I guess the issue is more that they are Republicans than they are evangelicals," she admitted, taking a long sip of green tea. "I mean, I'm a Jewish liberal from the Upper West Side. With these people I was just way out of context. I just didn't know who these people were."

ON A MUGGY September day in Washington, I joined a long line of white men and white women in front of the Treasury Building. These were Jewish Republicans, waiting patiently for a security check that would get them into the building, where the Republican Jewish Coalition was celebrating its twentieth anniversary with a gala luncheon whose main speaker would be President Bush.

"How many lunches does the guy eat every day?" asked a man behind me.

"Must be a couple," said his friend. "He has a lot of events."

"Jesus, he must get sick of it."

"Part of the job."

"I know, but he doesn't gain weight."

"Light lunches. He eats light lunches."

Standing in line I ran into Steve Emerson, the terrorism expert. Middle East maven Daniel Pipes was there. Someone called, "Make way for the Congressman" and Eric Cantor of Virginia walked past. Ask Republican pros who the Jewish comers are and they always mention Cantor and Senator Norm Coleman of Minnesota.

The ballroom was arranged with round tables, VIPs sitting above the crowd on a stage. Ken Mehlman, the chairman of the Republican National Committee, was up there, along with a smattering of Jewish legislators, a contingent of former ambassadors, and a few billionaires. Ari Fleisher was the MC; since leaving his job as Bush's spokesman he has become a political consultant for the Republican Jewish Coalition.

"Twenty years ago, 'Jewish Republican' was an oxymoron," Fleisher told the crowd. "We got eleven percent of the Jewish votes in the presidential race of 1992, we got sixteen percent in 1996, we got nineteen percent in 2000, and we went up to twenty-four percent this past election. That's called *inroads!*"

The Jewish Republicans cheered. Still, the pros in the room understood that inroads is what you get when you don't achieve real results. True, in 1992, George H. W. Bush won just 11 percent of the Jewish vote. But start counting in 1972, and you get a different trajectory. Nixon got a third of the Jews against McGovern, Reagan tickled 40 percent against Carter. By those measures, Dubya underperformed badly in 2004.

A Republican provided a brief invocation, and then, with no "Hail to the Chief," George Bush appeared on the stage and went right to the microphone, solving a mystery: at these lunches, he skips the food.

The president began with a eulogy to the recently departed Nazi hunter Simon Wiesenthal. "We stand with the victims of the Shoah," he proclaimed. Bush pronounced it *shoo-haw*. Clinton would have nailed it with a perfect Hebrew accent.

Bush's speech to the Jewish Republicans hit all the right notes on the fight against international terrorism and support for Israel. But you could tell his heart wasn't in it. Hurricane Katrina had just struck and Bush devoted much of his speech to that.

"Rabbi Stanton Zamek of the Temple Beth Shalom Synagogue in Baton Rouge, Louisiana, helped an African-American couple displaced by the storm track down their daughter in Maryland," recounted Bush. "When Rabbi Zamek called the daughter he told her, 'We have your parents.' She screamed out, 'Thank you, Jesus!' He didn't have the heart to tell her she was thanking the wrong rabbi."

The line got a laugh, but there was something off about it. For one thing, it is redundant to refer to a temple as a synagogue. For another, anecdotes featuring Jesus make Jewish audiences—even Jewish Republican audiences—uneasy. Bill Clinton would have known that, too.

Not long after the gala, I met Ken Mehlman at his red, white, and blue office. Mehlman was Bush's campaign manager in 2004, and he is still annoyed at his fellow Jews.

"A lot of them care about Israel last," he said. "Liberalism is their main concern, and they tend to hate anyone who isn't liberal. People like George Soros are self-hating Jews. Their instinct is to blame America first, and to blame Israel first."

I had been in Washington for several days, meeting with political analysts, all of whom seemed to feel that Bush's evangelical

Christianity had alienated Jewish voters. Mehlman agreed, but he put it down to bigotry. "A lot of what pisses Jews off about the religious right is just snobbery and ignorance," he said. "These are people who have never even met religious Christians. It's not about issues for them. Everything they see is through partisan hearts and minds. It's a generational thing. Jews were raised to be Democrats. We'll make inroads. Incremental inroads."

GEORGE W. BUSH is far more popular in Tel Aviv than he is in Washington. He's probably more popular in Tel Aviv than he is in Crawford. In the 2004 presidential election, among the forty thousand or so absentee ballots cast by Americans from Israel, about 70 percent were for Bush. Israeli public opinion polls showed a similar number of non-American Israelis favored the Republican candidate over John Kerry—despite the fact that Kerry had recently "discovered" that his grandparents were Jews and dispatched his brother to Israel to spread the news.

This Israeli-Republican affinity is relatively new. Through the 1960s, Israeli leaders usually preferred Democrats. Lyndon Johnson, in particular, was a great favorite of Prime Minister Levi Eshkol's. But, in 1972, when the McGovernites took control of the Democratic Party, things changed. Jerusalem was horrified by the dovish nature of McGovern's foreign policy and concerned by the large number of people around him who were, at best, tepid on the subject of Israel.

Israeli ambassador Yitzhak Rabin, with the blessing of Prime Minister Golda Meir, more or less openly campaigned for Richard Nixon in 1972 and helped him achieve about 40 percent of the Jewish vote.

By the time Jimmy Carter became president, in 1976, Rabin

was prime minister of Israel. Rabin came to Washington and dined at the White House. After the meal, President Carter invited him to go upstairs to say good night to his daughter, Amy. Rabin, who dreaded intimacy and didn't much care for children, said a curt no.

In 1977, shortly after his election, Menachem Begin traveled to Washington. He took the trip so seriously that he bought two new suits to replace the threadbare ones he had been wearing for years. He thought he was going to the United States to make history.

Begin's approach to Carter was the opposite of Rabin's. He turned on the charm, dwelled on their supposed mutual love of the Bible, and came back to Israel praising the president, calling him "the greatest man I have met since Ze'ev Jabotinksy." But Begin had misread Carter, who had been horrified by Begin's expansionist reading of the Old Testament and intended to do what was necessary to stop him from implementing it.

In November 1977, Egypt's Anwar Sadat shocked the world by coming to Jerusalem to meet Begin. The meeting had been prepared behind the backs of the Americans. Carter was furious and determined to take back control of Middle East diplomacy.

These events marked the start of a very nasty relationship between Carter and Begin. Carter labeled West Bank and Gaza settlements "illegal" and put opposition to them at the center of U.S. diplomacy. Carter saw that many liberal American Jews were themselves uneasy with Begin's settlement policy, and he used them, and the media, to paint Begin as a religious fanatic.

The strategy, like so many of Carter's strategies, failed. A lot of American Jews didn't like Begin, but they didn't like seeing Israel get beat up, either.

As relations between Washington and Jerusalem became more acrimonious (at one point Begin summoned the U.S. ambassador, Sam Lewis, and more or less publicly informed him that Israel was not an American-owned banana republic), Carter grew less and less popular with his Jewish constituents. In 1980, Ezer Weizman, Begin's former defense minister and bitter rival, campaigned for the president, but it didn't help much.

When Ronald Regan won in 1980, Begin was delighted. He admired Reagan's anticommunism. He had seen, and enjoyed, some of Reagan's movies (Begin had a taste for melodrama; he sometimes wept in the cinema). But most of all, Begin liked Reagan because he wasn't Carter.

Reagan stopped calling the settlements illegal. He gave tacit approval to the Israeli invasion of Lebanon in 1982 but stepped away from it when the television coverage of the Israeli bombing of Beirut turned American (and Israeli) public opinion. Still, while they didn't always agree, Begin never seriously questioned Reagan's essential support.

The warm feeling between the United States and Israel changed after Yitzhak Shamir became prime minister and George H. W. Bush came to the White House. Shamir was a hard-boiled, taciturn man, a hands-on former leader of the pre-Israeli right-wing Lehi terrorist group. Most of Shamir's career had been spent in the Mossad. He never believed that there was any prospect of peace and often cautioned against optimism: "The Arabs are the same Arabs, and the sea [they want to push us into] is the same sea," he often said. Shamir was determined to retain the West Bank and Gaza, not out of any religious sentiment (he was neither religious nor sentimental) but because he thought surrendering land would weaken Israel's defensive posture.

George H. W. Bush, for his part, was close, through his oil business connections, to the Saudi royal family (he called the Saudi ambassador, Prince Bandar, "Bandar Bush"). He was a mainline Christian, of the kind Bill Clinton later called "the frozen chosen."

And he was a foreign policy "realist." Bush had no feeling for Israel, and his secretary of state, James Baker, was even less sympathetic. During a disagreement with Israel over settlements and loans, he supposedly said, "Fuck the Jews, they don't vote for us anyway."

This was a self-fulfilling prophecy. In 1988, running against Dukakis as Reagan's heir, Bush received roughly 35 percent of the Jewish vote. In 1992, as his own man, he got just 11 percent, barely more than third-part candidate Ross Perot.

Republican Christian Zionists like Jerry Falwell supported Bush, but this didn't do him much good. The president was perceived by many evangelicals as patrician, high-church, and distant. Clinton was a Baptist, and if he was a sinner, at least he was a Southern boy, one of their own. The failure of Republican evangelicals to turn out in large numbers for Bush cost him the election. His attitude toward Israel almost certainly contributed to the general lack of born-again enthusiasm.

TONI MORRISON ONCE called Bill Clinton the first black president. He was certainly the first Jewish one. He discovered Jews at Georgetown and Oxford and Yale Law School—a rising meritocratic horde that was rapidly displacing the old WASP aristocracy in the country's elite liberal cultural, academic, and political institutions, including the Democratic Party—and made them Friends of Bill.

Clinton, with his déclassé background, could never pass for a WASP. But the Jews were delighted to befriend this big, good-looking all-American boy who didn't look down on them. Like them, Clinton was a usurper. Jews fell for him as hard as they had fallen for the Democratic nominee for president in 1952 and 1956, Adlai Stevenson (who, unlike Clinton, didn't love them back).

As president, Bill Clinton charmed both American Jews and Israelis. In 1994, when he appeared before the Knesset in Jerusalem, he gave a speech that could have come straight from Begin's friend Falwell.

"The truth is that the only time my wife and I ever came to Israel before today was thirteen years ago with my pastor on a religious mission," Clinton told the Israeli parliament. "I was then out of office. I was the youngest former governor in the history of the United States. . . .

"We visited the holy sites. I relived the history of the Bible, of your Scriptures and mine. And I formed a bond with my pastor. Later, when he became desperately ill, he said he thought I might one day become president. And he said . . . 'If you abandon Israel, God will never forgive you.' He said it is God's will that Israel, the biblical home of the people of Israel, continue forever and ever."

Some Israelis (me included) thought that Clinton laid it on a bit thick. But who, in the end, can turn down such devotion?

Clinton cultivated his relationship with Yitzhak Rabin, and used it to ease the very wary Israeli prime minister into his famous handshake with Yasir Arafat on the White House lawn. When Rabin was assassinated, in 1995, by an Israeli religious fanatic, Clinton seemed personally shaken. He came to the funeral in Jerusalem and stole the show with an eloquent eulogy, which ended with the Hebrew words *Shalom, chaver* ("Good-bye, friend"), a sentiment that became an instant bumper sticker in Israel.

Clinton got along much less well with Rabin's successor, Benyamin Netanyahu. If Rabin had been the father Clinton never had, Netanyahu was the competitive brother he couldn't stand. Both were young, smart, nakedly ambitious, charismatic, prone to woman trouble, and full of themselves. Netanyahu didn't like the Oslo Accords (which supposedly set the stage for a two-state peace deal) and dragged his feet as much as possible.

Netanyahu had been raised and educated in the United States and served as a senior diplomat in Washington and New York. More than any prime minister, he understood the dynamics of American politics. Did Clinton have the Jews in his pocket? Fine, Netanyahu would use the Republican evangelicals to stymie the American president and send a message to the liberal Jewish establishment as well; they were no longer necessarily Israel's closest American ally.

Netanyahu lasted only three years as prime minister, and he was followed by Ehud Barak of Labor. Clinton and Barak got along much better. They both wanted to cut a land-for-peace deal with Arafat. Barak, who had spent his entire life in the military, knew and cared very little about American politics. As it turned out, he didn't understand much about Israeli politics, either.

THE ELECTION OF George W. Bush in 2000 was a blow to the American Jewish community, which overwhelmingly supported Al Gore. It was also received with foreboding in Jerusalem, where Bush was seen as his father's son. In the 2000 election, Bush had been popular among Arab Americans and got a majority of their votes. Politically he owed the Jews nothing. There were no Jews in his cabinet or inner circle.

But Bush proved to be a very pleasant surprise. In March 2002, Palestinian bombers blew up a communal Passover seder at a hotel in the seaside resort city of Netanya. Thirty Israelis—mostly senior citizens—were killed, and another 140 were wounded. Prime Minister Ariel Sharon, who had meanwhile taken over for Barak, ordered the Israeli army back into the cities of the West Bank—which it had left under the Oslo agreements—with orders to destroy the terrorist infrastructure and isolate Yasir Arafat. The

Palestinian leader found himself holed up in his headquarters in Ramallah, where he remained until he died in 2004.

The Israeli operation was called *homat magen*—"defensive wall," a term that presaged Sharon's later decision to construct an actual physical barrier between Israeli settlements and the Palestinians. When the fighting started, President Bush sent Secretary of State Colin Powell to Israel, presumably to calm things down. Liberal Christian activists joined foreign policy "realists" in calling on Washington to force a cease-fire. But, barely six months after 9/11, the president of the United States was in for-us-or-against-us mode. So was Bush's evangelical base, which flooded the White House with e-mails and faxes supporting the Israelis. Bush, who clearly saw *homat magen* as an integral part of the war against Islamic radicalism, signaled to Sharon to go ahead and finish the job.

At the same time, Bush declared that he would support an independent Palestinian state next to Israel. He was, in fact, the first U.S. president bold enough to formally propose this, although it had been implied in the Oslo Accords. But, unlike his predecessors (including Clinton, who expected Israel to negotiate with the Palestinians during a terror war), Bush declared a new principle: Israeli concessions would be required *only* after the Palestinians stopped fighting.

Then, on June 24, 2002, the president stepped into the White House Rose Garden and called on the Palestinians to replace Yasir Arafat. This was like asking the New York Yankees to get rid of George Steinbrenner. Arafat, love him or hate him, owned the Palestinian franchise. Bush added that Arab states must act against anti-Israel terror or face the consequences.

Finally, in April 2004, following a meeting in Washington with Sharon, Bush completed a radical change in American policy by declaring that "realities on the ground" dictated that Israel should be allowed to keep some of its West Bank settlements. This reversed the position of every American government since the Six-Day War. It also cemented the born-again Bush's place as the most pro-Israeli president in the history of the United States.

It was growing more and more difficult for liberal American Jewish supporters of Israel—even those who hated Bush—to deny the positive role he and his Christian evangelical base were playing in Israel's security (and, by inference, theirs). Among the smarter and more farsighted Jewish leaders there were even second thoughts about the wisdom of demonizing the president and his core supporters, Americans who thought blessing Israel and supporting the Jews in a time of jihad should be an unshakable commitment of U.S. foreign policy.

TWELVE

ERIC IN WONDERLAND

Nine thousand kids packed the Vines Center at Liberty University on a Wednesday morning in April 2005. They were there to participate in a regularly scheduled convocation; most didn't realize that they would be attending a historic event. The speaker that day was Eric Yoffie. It was the first time in Liberty's history that a rabbi had been invited to address the student body.

Yoffie had never spoken to such a large group of evangelicals. And since I had seen an advance text of his remarks, I knew he was going to say things that had never before been said publicly at Liberty University.

Sitting in the audience among the students, I felt a twinge of anxiety. This had been my idea. A few months earlier, discussing the harsh attacks on evangelicals by Jewish leaders, Jerry Falwell had mentioned to me that he had never met Rabbi Yoffie. I suggested that it might be an interesting encounter, and he agreed. "I'd even invite him down here to talk with my students," Falwell said.

When I got back to New York I called Yoffie. Would he care to meet Jerry Falwell and give a talk at Liberty? At first, he thought I was kidding. When he realized I was serious, he promised to get back to me. Many of his colleagues, he discovered, opposed the idea of the head of the Reform movement appearing at Liberty University. But he decided to accept the invitation.

Now Yoffie's face was on giant monitors mounted around the Vines Center and his Massachusetts accent echoed through the normally honey-cured speakers. He had been given exactly eight minutes and his speech had been crafted to use every second of it.

He began by saluting evangelicals for their support of Israel. Then he highlighted their common ground for their opposition— as fellow religious people—to pornography, materialism, and no-strings-attached sex. "Who is at fault?" he asked rhetorically. "The Left, for confusing liberty with license and for ignoring public morality in the name of personal choice. And the Right, for being far too accepting of corporations that reach into our homes with their trash and relentlessly market sex and violence. I for one am sick and tired of media giants that tout family values in their news programs and press lewdness in their entertainment shows. Shame on all those who poison our public life in this way."

The students around me applauded. So far, so good.

Yoffie shifted into a brief lesson in American history.

The Founding Fathers of the United States were, Rabbi Yoffie told the students, "religious people who wanted God in public life. But they thought that religion must be a unifying force in America. They did not want government to be an agent of religion, and they refused to use sectarian language or images. It was they who authored the First Amendment, the noble sanctuary of our most precious freedoms."

Jerry Falwell is a Baptist and an advocate of the separation of church and state. The students applauded again.

Yoffie took a deep breath. "We can do all this without papering over our very real differences," he said. "Your religious tradition prohibits abortion; my religious tradition permits it in some cases and forbids it in others, but believes that every woman must prayerfully make the final decision for herself."

There was an audible intake of breath, but Yoffie barreled ahead. "You oppose gay marriage while we believe in legal protection for gay couples. We understand your reading of the biblical texts, even if we read those texts in a different way. But gay Americans pose no threat to their friends, neighbors, or coworkers, and when two people make a lifelong commitment to each other, we believe it is wrong to deny them the legal guarantees that protect them and their children and benefit the broader society."

This elicited a few hisses. I looked at Falwell on the platform, but his face was perfectly composed.

"As significant as these differences are, my hope is that they will not overwhelm us," said Yoffie. "We need less anger and more thoughtful reflection, less shouting and more listening. Even when we disagree, let's do so without demonizing each other. I can discuss these issues and believe what I believe without calling you a homophobic bigot, and you can do the same without calling me an uncaring baby killer. Let's promote respect for each other's religious tradition, and let's work for civility in public debate. And where we can, let's build bridges, find shared values, and join together in common cause."

Yoffie finished his speech to hesitant applause. Falwell rose and said, "I've spoken in synagogues where we had disagreements and I've never been booed. I want to thank Rabbi Yoffie for coming and speaking to us." The students understood the signal and applauded heartily. I did, too, relieved that my friend Eric was getting out of the Lynchburg lion's den in one piece.

After the speech, Falwell and Yoffie met the press. Yoffie said that he hoped this would be the beginning of a relationship between liberal Jews and evangelical Christians, and Falwell agreed.

"We can differ on many things not essential to the freedom of the country," he told journalists, adding that he wouldn't have asked the rabbi to travel all the way to Virginia if he hadn't been seeking a rapprochement.

FALWELL HOSTED A small private lunch after Yoffie's speech. The meal was, if not kosher, at least pork-free—a powerful culinary concession in a town whose best restaurant is called The Silver Pig. Yoffie confined himself to the vegetables, while Falwell tucked into a large plate of barbecue and rice. He's had heart problems lately, but it appears that he is relying on Jesus to be his cardiologist.

They made an incongruous pair sitting side by side at the round table: Falwell large and expansive, the graduate of a Missouri Bible college who now owns his own university and the mountain it sits on; Yoffie trim and laconic, a New Englander with a degree from Brandeis who rides a bicycle and reads Hebrew novels for recreation.

Grace was said. Then Yoffie thanked Falwell for his support for Israel. Falwell accepted this pleasantry without mentioning that he had been an ally of Israeli prime ministers when Yoffie was still a small-town congregational rabbi.

I asked Falwell a question I knew was on Yoffie's mind: Is evangelical support for Israel really an effort to bring about Armageddon? Falwell shook his head. "I believe absolutely in the Second Coming of Jesus," he said. "But I don't know when it will happen, and I don't imagine it will be anytime soon. In the meantime, protecting Israel is a practical matter. We need to do what's necessary to keep these Muslim barbarians from wiping it off the map the way they want to."

Yoffie blinked at the word "barbarian." Many American Jews, even some liberal Jews, feel the same way and say so in private conversations; still, nobody would utter such a thing out loud, to a stranger. But Falwell speaks his mind. At seventy-two, he had nothing to lose, and he was at the top of his political game. Senator John McCain who, a few years earlier, had called him an "agent of intolerance" was scheduled to come down to Liberty to deliver the university's commencement address. This was an admission that McCain needed Falwell in the GOP's Southern primaries. It was also a recognition that Falwell and his fellow evangelicals are, like it or not, a permanent part of the American political fabric.

The subject of Iranian nukes came up. Falwell confided that he thought George W. Bush was too politically constrained to do the right thing by taking out the ayatollah's reactors and Yoffie nodded; he shared that assessment.

Falwell took a sip of water. "So," he said, "it looks like the Israelis are going to have to do the job."

Yoffie sipped his own water and said nothing.

"Would you support them?" I asked Falwell.

"Not just me. The day Israel takes out the weapons of these barbarians, there will be eighty million evangelicals at the gates of the White House cheering. And I'll tell you something, President Bush will be cheering, too."

"How about your people?" I asked Yoffie. "Would they go to the White House?"

There was a long pause. Yoffie, the most important liberal rabbi in America, is a lifelong Zionist, but he is also an honest man. Finally he said, "That's a very good question. It would depend on the circumstances."

•   •   •

THIS EXPLAINS WHY the government of Israel has no intention of alienating its evangelical allies. Unconditional wartime support is a precious thing. Like Jewish Zionists, the evangelicals are influential, generous, and undemanding. But unlike the Jews, they are also impervious to accusations of neocon dual loyalty, unmoved by the need to seem evenhanded, and wholly indifferent to the good opinion of European sophisticates, progressive intellectuals, or the Palestinian enthusiasms of the mainline churches.

The Israel-evangelical seed planted by David Ben-Gurion during his appearance at the 1971 Jerusalem Prophecy Conference and nourished by Menachem Begin has now become a perennial. Evangelicals are in no sense exotic to Israeli leaders. The former Likud prime minister, Benyamin Netanyahu, has close connections with Pastor John Hagee. Ehud Barak, the former Labor prime minister, is a faculty member of Pat Robertson's Regent University. When Ehud Olmert came to office in 2006, his years as mayor of Jerusalem had put him on a first-name basis with just about every influential American evangelical leader.

But if the Israeli-evangelical connection is a fact, American Jews are still at the opening stages of a very tentative courtship. "Religiously, we have two basic problems with them," Yoffie told me before going down to Lynchburg, "Armageddon and conversion."

These may be valid theological differences, but have very little practical importance. American Jews are in no danger from Pentecostal proselytizers. They live in different worlds, cut off from one another by geography and social class. For the most part, evangelizers who deal with Jews are simply going through the motions. As for Armageddon, unless you actually believe in end times, what difference does it make what others believe? The premise of Armageddon is *passive*—it is brought about by God, and not by man. Are there evangelicals who think that Jesus is coming tomorrow? Sure, and there are Hasidim in Brooklyn who think the Lubavitcher Rebbe, the deceased head of the Chabad movement, is the Messiah. So what?

Some Jews are offended by Armageddon, because it makes them bit players in someone else's drama. But liberals in academia, the entertainment business, and the media need to be a little less self-righteous about this. They, too, promote an end-times utopia, a day when evangelical Bible-thumpers scrape the Confederate decals off their trucks and the mayonnaise off their sandwiches, beat their hunting rifles into sixteen-speed bicycles, replace Genesis with Darwin, and embrace Seinfeld values.

In any event, the greatest barriers to a Jewish-evangelical relationship are neither theological nor practical. Most Jews, like most evangelicals, embrace and practice middle-class family attitudes. Very few want their kids watching pornography or engaging in recreational sex. You won't find strip parlors in Jewish suburbs. Jews may oppose prayer in public schools, but they don't complain when the schools in their neighborhoods shut down on Rosh Hashanah and Yom Kippur. As any parent will admit in a truthful moment, Jews are not nearly as personally liberal on the subject of homosexuality as their public stance would suggest. And even unquestioning support for "abortion rights" is softening—at least for late-term procedures—under the graphic testimony of modern ultrasound.

This is not to say that there are no actual disagreements between the Jewish liberal mainstream and conservative evangelicals. There are, and will be. But the rhetorical gaps are much greater than the real differences.

To a large extent, American Jews, even after 350 years in the

New World, define themselves in opposition to Christians, as the people who don't go to church, get presents from Santa, or invoke Jesus. In recent years, they have also come to see themselves as sophisticated, upscale, ironic, Ivy League, even a bit European, with all that entails—very much including contempt for those who are not. Jews may not have landed at Plymouth Rock, but in recent decades they have made it to Martha's Vineyard, and they are sometimes not very sensitive to the feelings of the inhabitants of Gilligan's Island.

But that's changing. When Eric Yoffie returned from his visit with Jerry Falwell, he was deluged by messages from Reform rabbis and lay leaders from around the country. A few were angry, but most were highly positive. "I was taken aback by that," Yoffie told me a few days later. "On some level, I was amazed."

PART THREE

AFTERWORD: WARTIME

THIRTEEN

SUMMER CAMP

At the end of June 2006, my family and I went to Israel.
Annie, now nine, attended a day camp outside Tel Aviv.
Coby, ten, went off to his first sleepaway camp, at Michmoret, on
the shore of the Mediterranean, not far from Haifa.

Tel Aviv, when we arrived, was a big party. The cafés were full,
the beaches packed, the roads clogged with cars at two in the
morning as people headed to clubs and restaurants. The stock
market was up, business was good, and everyone talked about the
fact that Warren Buffett himself had just bought an Israeli company. Sure, a soldier had been captured in Gaza and rockets were
falling on a few border towns in the south, but they were small
towns and small rockets. Here and there, terrorists were caught
trying to infiltrate from the West Bank, which the public shrugged
off on a no-harm, no-foul basis. Ariel Sharon, the last great hero
of the War of Independence, had been felled by a massive stroke
and it was a sign of the country's mellow mood that he had been
replaced as prime minister by Ehud Olmert, a lawyer and politi-
cian with no military background and no charisma. Olmert
pledged to undertake an almost complete withdrawal from the
West Bank—a plan that would have been considered treasonous
by his mentor, Menachem Begin, and politically toxic only a few

years earlier. Pessimists fretted over the Iranian nuclear program, but the general sentiment was that the Bush administration could handle it, and anyway the issue would wait until after the World Cup finals in mid-July.

But on July 12, a Hezbollah commando unit crossed the northern border from Lebanon, attacked an Israeli patrol, killed eight soldiers, and took two more hostage. A barrage of Katyusha rockets hit the towns and farms of the Galilee. Prime Minister Olmert responded with a massive bombing of Hezbollah targets. Just like that, summer was over.

The Israeli battle plan was to wipe out Hezbollah from the air. But it became obvious it wouldn't work. Since Israel had left Lebanon unilaterally in 2000 (a withdrawal I supported), Iran and Syria had turned Hezbollah into a frontline infantry force. As Israeli planes futilely bombed well-built fortifications, hundreds of rockets rained down on northern Israel every day.

My son Coby was at camp when the war started, and at the end of his first week we drove up for a Saturday visit. It was a festive scene, hundreds of parents mingling on the lawn, munching pizza and listening to the skits and songs of the campers. The kids of a sister camp in the Galilee were there too, brought down to Coby's camp the day before to get them out of rocket range.

The camp director made it plain that he contemplated no change in schedule. "I doubt the missiles can reach us this far south," he said. "But if they do, we have shelters here. And we've been in touch with the civil defense authorities. Don't worry, things will be fine."

The next day, at five in the afternoon, we got a call from the director. There had been a change in the military intelligence assessment. The camp was now considered to be within Hezbollah's range (a couple of weeks later a missile struck not far away).

"We're calling off the session," he said. "Come get Coby right now."

Tel Aviv was also deemed within range. The government advised everyone in the metropolitan area to clean out their shelters, designate a safe room, and plan to run for cover in the event of an attack.

Lisa and I gave Coby and our daughter, Annie, a security briefing. They could play outside, but if they heard a siren they must race home. If they were too far away, they should take cover in a nearby building. "If an adult grabs you, go with him," Lisa said. Annie and Coby looked at each other with wide eyes; I thought of the expression in my older son Shmulik's eyes when I put a gas mask on him during the first Gulf War. Shmulik was a man now, a combat veteran of the intifada, finishing his first year in law school. He phoned his army reserve unit and asked why they hadn't called him up yet. Within a week, they did.

Saudi Arabia, Jordan, the Gulf states, and Egypt worried about the encroachments of Iran in Lebanon but, under pressure from their public opinion, fell into anti-Israel line. UN Secretary General Kofi Annan blamed Israel for "apparently" intentionally killing UN personnel in south Lebanon and spoke out against Israel's "disproportionate" response (in fact, Israel's response proved to be disproportionately mild; too mild to defeat Hezbollah, but that wasn't a goal of the UN). The Europeans predictably waffled; the French foreign minister even referred to Iran as a "stabilizing force" in the Middle East. The BBC and elite continental media judged Israel to be the aggressor.

None of this made much difference to Jerusalem; only the American attitude mattered. Some Israeli analysts predicted that Bush would soon force a halt to the fighting, which only proved that the pundits hadn't learned anything about the American president during the *homat magen* campaign three years earlier. Bush called Hezbollah the "root of the problem" and, unlike even his most pro-Israeli predecessors in the White House, saw to it that Israel had all the time it wanted. The president of the United States was not acting as an honest broker in this dispute, or even a dishonest one. He was flat-out pro-Israel.

Americans were, too. A *Los Angeles Times*/Bloomberg poll taken three weeks into the fighting showed 59 percent thought Israel was justified. Asked if, more generally, the United States should continue to side with Israel, 50 percent said yes. Only 2 percent said the United States should side more with Arab countries.

But the *LA Times*/Bloomberg poll also revealed a partisan gap. Two-thirds of Republicans said they favored continuing the alliance with Israel; only 39 percent of Democrats did. Most Democratic politicians around the country were vocally supportive of Israel; no one wanted to buck the party's Jewish establishment in a congressional election year. But it was a warning sign to Jewish liberal Zionists.

As usual, some of Israel's strongest critics were Jews. Congressman Bob Filner of California supported a cease-fire resolution that would have allowed Hezbollah to remain in place.

Adam Shatz, a literary editor at *The Nation,* compared Israel to the Nazis and Hezbollah to the French resistance. Rabbi Michael Lerner of *Tikkun* joined the National Council of Churches in a stance of "moral neutrality" between the Jewish state and its fascist enemies. A handful of Jewish "progressives" marched in Washington in an anti-Israel rally sponsored by the ANSWER coalition led by Ramsey Clark, the National Council of Arab Americans, and the Muslim American Society Freedom Foundation. The speaker's rostrum was decorated with a large banner, "Lebanon. Iraq. Palestine," which—unwittingly—made President Bush's point exactly: all three of those battlefields were part of the same war.

But these were marginal voices. Even mainstream American Jews who opposed war in Iraq were united behind the administration's support for Israel. In the 1982 war in Lebanon many Jewish liberals, influenced by the Israeli peace camp, had opposed the Begin government. But in 2006, Amir Peretz, a Labor Party peacenik, was the Israeli defense minister. When Human Rights Watch, headed by Kenneth Roth, undertook a crude, anti-Israel campaign, the group—normally the darling of liberal Jews—was denounced by every important Jewish organization in the country.

It fell to the Christian Zionists to hold the first major pro-Israel rally in Washington. This was an accident of timing. Reverend John Hagee's new group, Christians United For Israel, had scheduled its first national meeting for July 18. The war was only a week old when three thousand evangelical activists gathered at the Washington Hilton. The dais included Ken Mehlman, Jerry Falwell, Senators Sam Brownback and Rick Santorum, and the Israeli ambassador. Reverend Hagee gave a rousing speech in which he called the Bible "God's foreign policy statement" and made it clear that Israel's fight against Hezbollah was part of World War III. The next day, he sent his Christian soldiers to deliver that message to their congressional representatives.

American Jewish Zionists were upstaged once more when Pat Robertson showed up in Israel. Bombs fell as he broadcast *The 700 Club* from the town of Metulla, toured shelters in the Galilee, and visited Jerusalem. Forgiven by Israeli officials for his "God-smote-Sharon" crack, Robertson was warmly received by Prime Minister Olmert. The Pat reported that the two held hands and prayed, undoubtedly one of the harder moments of the war for the resolutely secular and deeply cynical Olmert.

Robertson also gave a long interview to the *Jerusalem Post,* in which he set forth his view of the conflict. "The Jews are God's Chosen People," he said. "Israel is a special nation that has a special place in God's heart. He will defend this nation. So evangelical Christians stand with Israel. That is one of the reasons I am here."

Robertson agreed with Bush, and Olmert, that the fight in Lebanon was part of a bigger war. "The nexus of this one comes out of Iran, which is ruled by a man who seems to be a wild-eyed fanatic," he said.

Robertson was asked if he told Olmert not to give up biblical land in the West Bank. "Olmert has been elected as the leader of Israel," Robertson said. "The Israelis have to be responsible for what their leaders do. It's up to them as a free society to determine the course of action of their nation. . . . I don't think the holy God is going to be happy about someone giving up his land. But that would be between Mr. Olmert and his God. It isn't for me to say. . . ."

WHILE PAT ROBERTSON was in Jerusalem, a man named Naveed Afzal Haq burst into the Jewish Federation office in Seattle, held a gun to the head of a thirteen-year-old girl, forced his way through security doors, and opened fire with two pistols. He shot six women. Five were wounded, including Danya Klein, who was pregnant. Another, Pat Waechter, died.

As Mr. Haq explained to a 911 operator, "These are Jews and I'm tired of getting pushed around and our people getting pushed around by the situation in the Middle East."

Following this incident, the *Forward*, voice of Upper West Side liberalism, flirted in an editorial with the possibility that there might actually be a jihad going on.

> The initial response to the Seattle shooting has been to treat it as something akin to an overheated domestic quarrel. The alleged shooter, Naveed Haq, is discussed as a mere misguided soul suffering from a toxic mix of ethnic prejudice and mental illness. That's how we responded to the deadly shooting attacks on the El Al desk at Los Angeles International Airport in 2002, on the observation deck of the Empire State Building in 1997, on Lubavitch students on the Brooklyn Bridge in 1994. Each was seen as an isolated act by a deranged individual. To think otherwise, to suspect that the shootings were part of a broad pattern of Muslim rage against Israel—a criminally violent response, that is, to actual Israeli actions—would be, in our minds, to legitimize the violence and blame the victim. We don't want to go there.
>
> That logic may have worked once, in an America of picket fences and Brotherhood Week. It does not make sense in a nation where colleges host "death to Israel" rallies, where movie stars and university deans publicly blame Israel and the Jews for America's troubles. In today's incendiary atmosphere, it does not take an organized conspiracy to create a concrete threat to American Jews. The nature of the threats has changed. It is time for a change in the response.

And what should the new response be? Did the *Forward* call on young Jews to join the fight, enlist in the army or the CIA or the FBI? Did it demand more stringent surveillance of radical Islamic movements in the United States? No, the *Forward*, speaking for the Jewish left, didn't want to go there.

Instead, it put the onus on Israel.

"We proclaimed to the world that we and Israel are one," the paper said ruefully.

> It may once have been true that Israel's policies were only Israel's business, but no longer. In this new, interconnected world, American Jews now share the costs of Israel's actions. We are entitled to have our interests represented at the table where decisions are made. If the organizations that purport to represent American Jews will not speak for us, then someone else must be found who will do the job.

Reading the editorial, I wondered what Professors Mearsheimer and Walt would make of the idea—American Jews sitting around the cabinet table of the Israeli government in Jerusalem deciding policy.

IN THE MEANTIME, the Jewish community geared up for fundraising. The United Jewish Appeal, now known as the United Jewish Communities, began an emergency fund that brought in upwards of $170 million in one month. But the real financial news of the war was supplied by Yechiel Eckstein.

Eckstein filmed a commercial, featuring missiles firing, blaring sirens, a fearful Israeli woman, and an 800 number and tried to buy airtime on the three cable news networks. CNN and MSNBC turned him down, but Fox agreed. As soon as the ads hit the air it became apparent that Eckstein had, once more, turned on the golden spigot.

The normal expectation for a televised appeal is 80 cents on the dollar; the other 20 cents and a profit come in follow-up solicitations. Eckstein didn't get 80 cents. He got $3.00, an almost unheard-of response. On August 8, an internal memo of the International Fellowship of Christians and Jews reported, "We are up to *145.1 percent* of last year at this time."

Eckstein's ads were airing in the United States at the end of July, when we returned from Israel. More than a year had passed since I had seen Pastor Steve Munsey ride his Harley onto the pulpit at the Family Christian Center in Indiana. Since then I had chatted with members of the biblical tribe of Manasseh in the Armageddon grocery store, lunched with a woman who raises the dead, fellowshipped with Jerry Falwell, and floated on the Sea of Galilee with a guy named Catfish. Sue Ricksecker, the church secretary from Pontiac, kept sending me books, including a rare copy of *Famous Hebrew Christians,* with a chapter on Hyman Appleman; presumably I was still on her cell phone conversion list. I had talked Jewish politics with Ken Mehlman and The Professional, toured Pat Robertson's Virginia headquarters, met a born-again Hollywood producer on an angel-hunting expedition in Denver, and spent countless hours trying to explain to my friends and relatives what on earth I was looking for.

I had been looking for confirmation that making common cause with the Republican evangelical "enemy" was both safe and prudent—and the war in Lebanon confirmed it. Israel's security now depends on this coalition, just as a viable Jewish diaspora depends on Israel's continued well-being. And, in the clutch of jihad, that coalition is proving itself.

Baffled European elites can't imagine anyone really liking Israel, a country that the French ambassador in London, in a moment of exasperated candor, once described as a "shitty little country." But thanks to Christian Zionists—foremost among them George W. Bush—support for Israel had become not a Jewish special interest, or even a short-term strategic partnership, but a bilateral, bicultural, all-American fact of life.

FOURTEEN

YES FOR AN ANSWER

A fact, not a given. There are no final victories in the affairs of nations, no eternal alliances, and nothing's free. Evangelicals may be, as Yechiel Eckstein says, "pure," and they may support Israel for biblical reasons. But there is more than one way to read the Bible, and every self has interests.

A month into the war in Lebanon, an enterprising Associated Press reporter, Rachel Zell, noticed a strange silence where declarations of support for Israel should have been. She called three major evangelical groups—Focus on the Family, the Southern Baptist Convention, and the National Association of Evangelicals—and asked why they had refrained from publicly supporting the Jewish state.

James Dobson, head of Focus on the Family, reacted immediately by issuing a statement comparing Israel with "little David" up against "mighty Goliath" and labeling Hezbollah the aggressor. "While we are praying without ceasing for the innocent victims in Lebanon, we stand firmly with Israel and the Jews," he said.

Richard Land, the SBC's man in Washington, who had appeared at Yechiel Eckstein's Stand For Israel conference the previous fall, was a little softer. "Southern Baptists overwhelmingly support Israel's right to live at peace with her neighbors and pray for the peace of Jerusalem to prevail in the Middle East," he said. Lebanon and Hezbollah went unmentioned.

The most interesting reaction belonged to Ted Haggard, president of the National Association of Evangelicals. Haggard admitted that the Israeli government had been pressuring him to make a statement of support, and he had refused.

"Our silence is not a rejection of Israel or even a hesitation about Israel. Our silence is to try to protect people," he explained to Zell. "There's a rapidly growing evangelical population in virtually every Islamic country. Much of it is underground in the countries that are more radicalized, and many of the Christians survive based on their neighbors' just ignoring the fact that they don't go to mosque."

This sounded like something the mainstream Protestant denominations might say. Was the National Association of Evangelicals really more concerned with their institutional interests in the Middle East than with God's covenant with Abraham? Did this signal a departure, a turn away from Christian Zionism by the country's largest evangelical umbrella group?

When I called Reverend Haggard in Colorado Springs, he was at first polite but guarded.

"Of course, evangelicals are supportive of Israel," he told me. "Two terrorist groups attacked Israel. I didn't speak out immediately because we needed some time to move some people around, that's all. There are evangelical Christians in just about every totalitarian nation in the Middle East, over there trying to help out. In the era of universal media, some sixteen-year-old fanatic in a village might hear or read some statement I make, pick up a machine gun, and kill a nun or a missionary. Some other evangelical leaders have made disparaging statements in the past about Muslims that have made it really difficult for our people. Every day, around the world, four hundred eighty Christians are martyred. We try to minimize that. So there is a possible clash between our principled argument for Israel and safety of Christians. But I want to make it clear: we are unequivocal in our support for Israel."

That seemed to clarify matters, but Haggard had more to say. He was, it turned out, still smarting from Mikey Weinstein's charges—now wending their way through the courts in the form of a lawsuit—that evangelicals at the Air Force Academy discriminate against Jews.

"The scandal at the academy was way overrated," he said. "I hired a legal team to investigate, and they reported that there *were* some things over the line—like the football coach's banner—but they were dealt with under the standing rules of the academy. What Weinstein wants to do is to force the chaplains to pray according to government supervision. This is the first time in American history that anyone has petitioned a court to supervise the words and actions of military chaplains. If he wins, it will amount to the establishment of religion in America, religion approved by the state."

I told Haggard that I had read his e-mail exchange with Weinstein.

"Then you know who I'm dealing with," he said. "I published the correspondence so people could see the way he thinks and expresses himself."

Haggard was especially upset that Weinstein had implied he might be anti-Semitic. "Historically Christians, all kinds of Christians, did horrible things to the Jews. It's only since the establishment of the state of Israel that a structural effort has been made to right that wrong. All my Christian lifetime I've heard that the Jews are God's Chosen People, that those who bless the Jews will be blessed. My generation was highly motivated to unconditionally support the state of Israel, *because* it is a Jewish state."

"Right," I said. "Well, I've enjoyed talking to you. . . ."

"But I'm worried," said Haggard. He no longer sounded guarded. "A new megachurch goes up in this country every three weeks. These are evangelical churches, filled with young people. My fear is that they don't believe they should support Israel unconditionally. They look at someone like Mikey Weinstein or hear what Abe Foxman says about evangelicals and they think, These people are my enemy.

"The Israelis need to know this," he said. "They need to intensify their relationship with us, but mainly they need to communicate with American Jews, tell them that they should stop attacking us."

Why go through Israel? I asked. Why not communicate directly to the American Jewish leadership?

Haggard seemed surprised. "We don't speak the same language," he said. "After Abe Foxman said what he said about evangelicals, I asked for a meeting, but it never took place. He didn't want to meet. And every other time I've suggested Jews do anything, the Jewish newspapers in New York have just been *appalled*. During the controversy over *The Passion* I stated my opinion about the movie, and I was treated with disrespect. So I've decided to just stay quiet. I'm a pastor, not a warrior."

"Mikey Weinstein, Abe Foxman, and some reporter at a Jewish newspaper, *that's* who's upsetting you?"

"Absolutely," he said. "Look, if evangelicals step out of line, like Pat Robertson did when he called for the assassination of the president of Venezuela, we speak out. Jews ought to do the same thing. If Abe Foxman says outrageous things about us, it shouldn't be up to us to argue with him. It should be up to the other Jewish organizations. But we're very interested in the silence of the Jewish groups and leaders.

"Look," Haggard said, "I'm going to support Israel no matter what. That's how I was raised; it's what I believe. But if this continues, I'm fearful of the rise of anti-Semitism. For the past twenty years Jews have had an opportunity to respond to the friendliness of evangelicals and they haven't. I can't stand the kind of vitriolic language I get, and you can imagine how it goes over with young evangelicals in the Christian blogosphere. We have to be sensitive to one another, and that means Jews have to learn how to tolerate evangelical Christians, too. I don't want to live in an America where Jews and Christians are enemies."

JEWS AND EVANGELICALS are major stakeholders in opposing parties. But the Judeo-Christian bargain doesn't require Jews to become Republicans, much less Christians. It simply requires a change in attitude and tone, what Eric Yoffie meant when he said that it was time for Jews to stop dismissing tens of millions of their fellow Americans as "bigots."

As I was finishing this book, I got a message from an old friend, a writer I respect who read an early draft. He thought I was being too easy on the evangelicals. "I believe you might be pulling your attitude in the name of fairness, journalism, balance, whatever," he wrote. "I mean, can you get pissed off about these people horning in on a good thing in Israel? These are the same people, after all, who would sell Jews down the river. These are the good neighbors of Berlin in 1943, no?"

I don't think they are. I looked hard for evidence that the evangelicals are insincere, cynical, or devious in their attitude toward Israel and the Jews, and I didn't find it. They may love Jews too much. They may love Jews for the wrong reasons. They may, in the future, not love Jews at all. But for now, the evangelical Christians of America are not the enemy. They are the enemy of the enemy, and they want to be accepted and appreciated. In return they are offering a wartime alliance and full partnership in a Judeo-Christian America. It is an offer the Jews of America should consider while it is still on the table.

ACKNOWLEDGMENTS

A great many people helped me with this book. Thanks are due to my agent, Flip Brophy, at Sterling Lord Literistic; my editor, David Hirshey, who believed in the project and steered me through it; Nick Trautwein; and Kate Hamill.

Several friends (and one daughter) read and critiqued the manuscript. Thanks to Michal Chafets, Brett O'Donnell, Malcolm MacPherson, and Rick Marino. All contributed to the making of this book. None are responsible for its shortcomings or its opinions.

A lot of people gave me their time and their help. I especially want to thank Rabbi Yechiel Eckstein, who opened the world of the International Fellowship of Christians and Jews to a some- times uncomfortable scrutiny; and IFCJ staffers Joan Watson, George Mamo, Dvero Ganani, and Reverend Jerry Clark. Thanks are also due to Rabbi Eric Yoffie, Reverend Dan Stratton, Rever- end Ann Stratton, Reverend Jerry Falwell, Gary Bauer, Rabbi David Saperstein, Ari Fleischer, Mark McKinnon, Ken Mehlman, Professor Charles Dunn, Professor John Green, Gary Rosenblatt, Judith Shulevitz, Reverend Bill Wilson, Reverend Connie Wilson, Reverend Tom Malone, Sue Ricksecker, Greg Menken, Ira Foreman, Dr. David Elcott, Ethan Felson, John Harris, Don Egle, Shira Dicker, Rabbi Tom Gutherz, Alexander Rechter, Duke Westover, Jerry Benjamin, Reverend Joe Atavai, Noga Tarnopolsky, Jay Lefkowitz, and Megan Lieberman of the *New York Times Magazine*. Most of all, thanks and love to Lisa Beyer.

INDEX